NOW RINGS THE BELL

NOW RINGS THE BELL

The Story of Ralph Jacobs
Missionary Pioneer to Africa

by
ESTHER EMBREE

Light and Life Press
Winona Lake, Indiana 46590

Printed in the United States of America
by Light and Life Press
Winona Lake, Indiana
46590

Copyright © 1978 by
Light and Life Press
ISBN 0-89367-023-5

All rights reserved. No part of this book may be reproduced in any form, except for brief quotations in reviews, without the written permission of the publisher.

Dedication

Dedicated to the courageous African Free Methodist pastors in Rhodesia who are faithfully continuing the work of evangelism begun by Ralph Jacobs.

May they always "be filled with his [God's] mighty, glorious strength so that [they] can keep going no matter what happens — always full of the joy of the Lord ..." (Colossians 1:11, *The Living Bible*).

CONTENTS

Chapter 1. Southern Rhodesia, 1928   9
Chapter 2. Portuguese East Africa, 1928   13
Chapter 3. Youngsville, Pennsylvania, 1888-1915   15
Chapter 4. South Africa, 1916-1919   23
Chapter 5. Portuguese East Africa, 1919-1938   29
Chapter 6. Southern Rhodesia, 1939-1955   73
Chapter 7. United States, 1955-1970   115
Epilogue, 1956-1977   121
Appendixes:
    Say It This Way   124
    Missionaries in Mozambique and
        South Africa (excluding Transvaal)   125
    Missionaries in Rhodesia   128

The Sengwe bell, now broken, was made into a cairn by Dr. Embree in 1967.

Evangelist Samueli loved the word of God.

Chapter 1

Southern Rhodesia 1928

An air of quiet excitement spread quickly through Chief Sengwe's kraal as two travelers approached the edge of the clearing and called in greeting. Skinny dogs barked. Drowsy villagers, resting from the morning labor, were suddenly alert. Even the wind awakened and busied itself among the leaves of the kanya trees, while from behind their mothers' skirts, tiny children watched wide-eyed as the men were welcomed into the village with simple, solemn handshakes. There was no outward show of emotion, yet the joy of reunion filled every heart and was understood by all. Tonight there would be celebration. The sons of the chief had returned home from far away.

Many seasons had passed in this remote southeast corner of Southern Rhodesia since the young men had left on their 450-mile walk to find work in the mines of Johannesburg. Those who traveled so far did not always return. This Shangaan chief's family had wondered often, as they sat talking around their fires at night, whether they would ever see or hear from their young men again. But today they were home, safe.

Their shoulders had broadened and their faces had matured. Their loinskins had been replaced by fine, cloth trousers and shirts. The bright-colored suitcases they brought home on their heads were sure to be full of white man's wonders. But what was that curious, heavy black simbi (iron) they had carried suspended from a pole across their shoulders? Indeed, there would be remarkable stories told around the fire tonight!

However, important matters must not be discussed until the stomach is satisfied. The herd boys scurried off to capture a goat from the family flock. The girls went hurrying to the river with their waterpots, and the women chattered happily as they prepared the evening meal of wuŝa and xixewu (porridge and gravy). Some of them cooked the goat meat into savory gravy, flavoring it with peanuts and greens. Others ground millet into fine, smooth flour, between two flat rocks, then cooked it to thick, steaming perfection in a black pot over an open fire.

At last the food was ready. The wives respectfully served the men first, then retreated the proper distance to wait for them to finish. The women would eat their share with the children.

When the men were satisfied, the women brought them a basin of water to wash the sticky porridge from their fingers. The glowing coals were coaxed into flame, and as the firelight illuminated the circle of eager faces, Chief Sengwe leaned back with a contented sigh and opened the conversation by inviting his sons to speak. From the shadows, the women strained to catch their words. Women were not permitted to sit near the men, not even on such an important occasion as this.

In unhurried fashion, the young men recounted their story, beginning with the morning two years before when they had left home on their long walk. They had carefully rehearsed every detail in their memories so they could tell the family on their return. Bit by bit, punctuated by exclamations from the spellbound audience, they told it now, as only a Shangaan can tell a story. Several hours passed, and the lazy fire was poked awake again and again. The listeners did not grow sleepy.

At the proper time, the suitcases were opened and the gifts from the white man's city were given and received with soft, thankful clapping of the hands. Finally, the chief pointed toward the heavy, black simbi. "Tell us about that," he said.

His sons explained how a white Mufundisi (teacher) had come to their mine compound, preaching about the Great Spirit who loves everyone. He had read to them from a special book and taught them songs about the Great Spirit. This had reminded them of another white Mufundisi who used to live on the hill at Sengwe when they were small children. That man had also talked about the Great Spirit. But before the people could fully understand his message, he had become sick with fever and had to return home across the Great Water. Although the people had waited and hoped, no one else ever came to take his place. Only the white man's name and the date remained in the baobab tree where he carved them before he left.

But there in the big city, when they heard the message again, they had remembered. And they remembered how their father had often told them of his desire for a missionary to come to Sengwe. Now they, too, wanted their family back home to hear the message. However, they saw that in the big city the white man always used a large iron bell to worship his God; and a bell always called the white children to school. So, they reasoned, if only they had a white man's bell at Sengwe, then, perhaps, a missionary would come and teach them.

With that plan in mind, they saved their money until they had enough (six pounds or eighteen dollars) to buy a bell. When they were ready to return home, the bell rode with them on the white man's iron horse as far as the small town of Zook Makar. From there they walked four days (more than one hundred miles), carrying the heavy bell suspended from a pole across their shoulders. They saw elephants often. Once they saw lion. Sometimes, when they were thirsty, there was no water. Always the bell was heavy, but they did not give up. Does not the Shangaan proverb say, "Even a rabbit becomes heavy before you reach home"?

When their story was finished, the chief nodded his approval. Then, while everyone watched, he walked to the bell and moved the heavy iron handle slowly back and forth. Its clear, resonant tones resounded through the hushed village and out across the surrounding countryside. "It is good," the chief declared. "Now, who will come and teach us what it says?"

Chief Sengwe was thoughtful before he spoke again. Then he said that while his sons were away, a man named Samueli had visited the village of Pafuri, in the land of the Portuguese, a day's journey from Sengwe. Samueli had also preached about this Great Spirit, and he said he had learned about Him from Mufundisi Jacobi, a white man who lived near the Great Water. Perhaps, the chief suggested, if they asked Mufundisi Jacobi, he would send someone to teach in their village.

Returning to his place by the fire, Chief Sengwe ordered his counselor to write a letter. Then, as he spoke, the counselor slowly formed the words on a scrap of paper.

To Mufundisi Jacobi:

I greet you. I have heard from your evangelist, Samueli, that you teach people about God. We have no one to teach us. I am weeping to see the people perish. Oh, hurry and send us a missionary. We have bought a bell.

It is I,
Chief Sengwe.

The counselor folded the paper carefully, walked to the edge of the village and broke a small branch from a tree. He stripped it of leaves and cut a thin slit in one end. Into the slit he fitted the letter firmly. The message was ready.

Calling a messenger, the chief instructed him: "Take this and go to the village of Pafuri. Wait there until Samueli comes again. Give him my letter and ask him to take it to Mufundisi Jacobi. We will wait for his answer."

Chapter 2

Portuguese East Africa 1928

Mr. Jacobs smiled broadly as he opened the door wide to welcome Samueli into his office at Inhamaxafo Mission Station in Portuguese East Africa. Samueli had just returned from the land of the vaHlengwe, far to the west, where Portuguese East Africa borders Southern Rhodesia. It was 1928, and for several years Mr. Jacobs had been sending African volunteer evangelists (pastors) on what he called "spying-out" missions to explore new areas, preach the Word, and bring back reports of the country, the people, and of suitable places to extend the work. He was eager now to hear what Samueli had found. But first, they must exchange greetings and enjoy the ever-welcome, unhurried cup of tea. At last Mr. Jacobs motioned Samueli to speak.

The story he told of his three-hundred mile trip to the western border was full of action, adventure, and hardship. Samueli had slept in trees at night when lions were about. Once he had escaped from an angry rhino by waiting until the rhino lowered its head to charge, then dodged out of its way and ran fast. The two men laughed together before Samueli continued. Mr. Jacobs wanted most to hear about the people and their needs, and Samueli told of finding many who lived in darkness, without having heard the news of Jesus. Only the men who worked in the mines were hearing about Jesus from missionaries there. Back home in their remote villages, there was no one to tell the good news of Jesus. Yet, Samueli said, the people were ready and willing, even eager to listen. Some begged him to stay longer and teach them more. In fact, a Chief Sengwe, who lived across the border in Southern Rhodesia, had heard of Samueli's previous visit to Pafuri and sent a letter to the Mufundisi asking for a missionary to come and teach his people. With that, Samueli handed Mr. Jacobs the travel-worn, cleft stick with the letter still firmly in place.

Carefully Mr. Jacobs smoothed out the paper and looked at the smudged words that had been written weeks before. They were difficult to make out, but when he had finished reading, their message was loud and clear. His heart was moved in response to Chief Sengwe's request. He could almost hear the bell ringing — "a mere tinkling cymbal" — without someone to translate its message of love. His heart wept, too, for those waiting to hear. He wanted to go. Had God not called him to pioneer in places where people had never heard? This remote, southeastern corner of Southern Rhodesia was just such a place, and he already knew the language of the vaHlengwe people. He would pray God to open the door and make it possible to answer Chief Sengwe's call.

Mr. Jacobs did not know it would be ten long years before that door would open.

Chapter 3

Youngsville Pennsylvania 1889-1915

It's a boy!" The joyous news spread excitement as it passed from house to house through the usually placid town of Youngsville, Pennsylvania, on that brisk morning of October 1, 1889. This was not just another baby. This was the first child of the young, successful, and much-loved country doctor.

In their rambling, white frame, two-storied home, Dr. Jacobs and his wife, Belle, welcomed their tiny son with thanksgiving and named him Ralph Jackson Jacobs. They could not know, nor even imagine, the far-off places to which he would go, nor the extent of his influence in years to come.

Those who remember, say that Ralph was a happy, ordinary child with the usual amount of naughtiness which brought him the usual amount of punishment. They also say that he possessed the rare ability to turn his punishments into advantage. For example, when his mother tied him to a tree for running away from home, he changed his game to "horsey" and used the rope for "reins." This characteristic did not leave him when he matured; but all through his life, Ralph viewed obstacles as "opportunities with challenge."

One of Ralph's favorite boyhood haunts was Brokenstraw Creek, which meandered across their backyard on its way through the center of town. By its banks, under the willow and mulberry trees, Ralph learned the joys of fishing and the wonders of nature. In floodtimes, the creek's wild waters provided ample excitement and adventure. In the hills that surrounded their valley community, Ralph and his father hunted rabbit, deer, fox, and bear. Without question, Ralph was happiest when out-of-doors.

It was Ralph's responsibility to keep his father's horse and buggy ready to make house calls at any time; and as a reward, he was sometimes allowed the privilege of accompanying him on a hurried trip into the country.

For thirteen years, Ralph enjoyed life as an only child, and he was not expecting a change in status. It is no wonder, then, that when the second and last child, Howard Charles, was born, Ralph reacted by disappearing for the day to go fishing.

Dr. and Mrs. Jacobs were both active and popular in the social life of their tiny town. Charles was a member of the Odd Fellows. Belle was a Rebekah. In keeping with their social standing, the family attended the Methodist church, the largest church in Youngsville.

The direction of their lives took a sudden and dramatic turn when Belle was soundly converted in an old-fashioned revival meeting and moved her membership to the unfashionable, white frame Free Methodist Church down in the next block. This unexpected action stirred the entire town and brought criticism from many of her friends who did not understand. Even Charles opposed her, but though she was small in stature, Belle was determined of mind and could not be swayed from what she believed to be the will of God.

A short time later, the town was shaken again when Dr. Jacobs became ill with appendicitis. Surgery was performed, but peritonitis had already set in. The year was 1905. Antibiotics were as yet unknown. There was no way to control the infection, and in a few days Ralph's father was dead, at the age of forty-nine. However, before he died, he too acknowledged Christ as His Saviour.

The following year, seventeen-year-old Ralph, his

mother, and his three-year-old brother, packed a few belongings and took the train to Greenville, Illinois, where Ralph enrolled in a business course at Greenville College. Ralph had only one ambition — to be a farmer in the Yakima Valley, Washington.

During the school's fall revival, under the ministry of the Reverend H. C. Morrison, a Southern Methodist preacher, Ralph was moved to make his own personal commitment to Jesus Christ. That experience brought him to the realization that perhaps God had another plan for his future. As he explained it:

> ... When I was converted, I immediately felt that the bottom had dropped out of my plan for my life. ... The great cry of my heart was for God to show me concerning my life's work. This continued for several years until one day during my schooling at Greenville, while in secret prayer, I heard the Lord speak as plainly as though by an audible voice, saying, 'I want you in Africa!' I immediately arose from my knees, went into the sitting room where my mother was, and told her that the Lord had called me to Africa. ...

During the months before, while Ralph was struggling with his future, Belle was concerned that whatever his problem, he would obey God. While she was praying for him one day, a multitude of black faces appeared before her, and she assumed God was calling her to be a missionary in Africa. In great astonishment, she told the Lord she was too old to go and totally unprepared. God replied that He was not calling her, but her son. Belle waited until Ralph came to tell her of his own call to Africa before she shared her vision with him, and then they wept and rejoiced together over the way God was leading in his life.

At school that year, Ralph's roommate, George D. Schlosser, was also preparing for mission work. George's friendship was especially strengthening, and Ralph needed all the strength he could get. Rich Uncle Fred was trying to discourage his nephew from making what he considered to be a terrible mistake. He offered to buy a farm in the Yakima Valley, stock it completely, and give it to Ralph, paid-in-full, if only he would forget about Africa. Ralph would not forget.

Having made his decision, Ralph sent his application to the Mission Board of the Free Methodist Church, requesting an assignment in Africa. He was so sure Africa was the right place, that when the Board asked if he would go to Osaka Bible School in Japan, he refused. He had already learned to recognize God's voice and to obey in simple faith. Even before he received an appointment, Ralph was busy preparing himself for service in Africa. On his application form, dated 1909, he wrote:

> ... During the past summer, I have studied Zulu and have sent my lessons to J. P. Brodhead. (Brodhead was a missionary serving in South Africa at that time.)

Others began to notice Ralph's missionary interest. One was his professor, C. A. Stoll, who wrote in his recommendation of the candidate:

> ... One of the best students in college ... his physical and mental fitness, his tactfulness, his passion for souls. ... He is of quiet disposition but keeps active in aggressive home missionary work. ...

On completion of his college course, Ralph returned with his family to Youngsville and apprenticed himself to a mason, Henry Lightner. Before long, Ralph's attention was turned to the boss's daughter, a pretty, bright-eyed girl with a warm smile and wavy, chestnut hair. Ralph had known Ethel Mae all his life. They had grown up in the same little town, attended the same country school and church. In fact, it was Ralph's father, Dr. Jacobs, who had attended her birth, and on that day had been heard to remark, "She's certainly a fine girl, but we have a fine boy at our place." That "fine boy" was just beginning to notice what a "fine girl" Ethel was.

One evening after church, Ralph asked Ethel, "May I walk you home?" Ethel replied, "No, thank you, I can walk home quite well by myself." Turning to her younger sister, Ralph said, "Well, I'm sure Mary, here, would like someone to walk her home." With that, he took an arm of each girl and escorted both of them. Ralph and Ethel's friendship developed rapidly after that, and they were soon engaged.

Ralph's marriage proposal was much more than flowery words. Ralph asked Ethel to share not only his love and his life, but his work as a pioneer missionary. And that, he said, would include primitive living conditions and unknown dangers. Ethel, however, was prepared for the challenge. She had dedicated her life for missionary service when just a young girl, and she was willing now for the rugged life Ralph proposed.

Ethel was the second child in a family of six children — three boys and three girls. Like Ralph, Ethel had absorbed the wholesome environment of a farm community, and she shared his love of the outdoors. Hers was an adventurous spirit. Her sense of humor was a gift that would see her through much unpleasantness and hardship. Her graciousness would often make a tent into a home. Her willingness to be content, whatever the situation, and her devotion to her Lord, would keep her happy while adjusting to all the changing circumstances they were to encounter.

Their wedding took place in Ethel's home on April 12, 1911, performed by the Reverend A. H. M. Zahniser. Careful plans had been laid so that following the ceremony, they were dashed away in a horse and buggy to the railway station from where they left on a short honeymoon.

Five months later, both of them enrolled in Greenville College to take the two-year course recommended for missionary candidates.

One day while they were at Greenville, Ethel was watching a beautiful baby and thinking about the family she hoped to have; but God seemed to say to her, "Babies are not for you, Ethel." Ralph had already felt that being in pioneer work would make it difficult for them to give children proper care and attention. Ralph and Ethel both loved children, but without complaint, they accepted God's plan and purpose in this part of their lives. Although they were never given children of their own, other missionaries' children, through the years, learned to love them as "Aunty Ethel and Uncle Jakey," and countless babes were born into the kingdom of God through their ministry.

In the spring of 1913, the young couple was ready for appointment, but Mother Jacobs was ill. Without Ralph, there would be no one to look after her except ten-year-old Howard. A delay was approved, and Ralph spent the time in further preparation by continuing to work for Mr. Lightner. In addition, he and Ethel chose to live in a large tent during that summer, using few conveniences, just to accustom themselves to African living.

By the time Mother Jacobs had recovered, World War I was making overseas travel inadvisable, so a second year of waiting was necessary. Ralph was appointed pastor of the difficult Van circuit, with three preaching points, which kept them busy traveling the area by horse and buggy, and paid an inadequate salary. But besides the generous amounts of meat and vegetables they received from grateful parishioners, they also gained valuable pastoral experience.

Ralph and Ethel were finally appointed to South Africa on October 27, 1915. The following excerpt of a letter, written to Ralph by the missionary secretary, is the only glimpse we have of the difficulties they must have encountered packing for seven years of overseas living.

October 18, 1915

... In regards to that flour sack full of dried apples; it will be all right for you to take them with you, but you must not try to take them in a flour sack. You should secure tin cans that can be closed tightly and pack them in these. Otherwise, they will be spoiled on the way....

On the day they left home, December 2, 1915, their hometown paper carried the headlines, **They Have Made the Supreme Sacrifice.** Beneath their picture was a two-column article about South Africa and the work Ralph and Ethel would be doing. It was evident that the entire community respected and admired their courage and dedication.

A large group of family and church friends gathered at the depot to farewell them with songs, prayers, and tears. Howard was certain he would never see his big brother again. In his twelve-year-old imagination, Africa was out of this world.

The train took them to New York; and two days later, Ralph and Ethel were sailing for Liverpool. Traveling the sea in wartime was uncertain at best (their ship, the S.S. *New York,* was sunk later in the war), but they arrived only two days late, due to stormy weather. The vessel they had expected to take on to Durban, had been commandeered to transport troops, so they found passage instead on the *Royal Mail* steamer. That was a faster ship, but even so, it was forty-four days from the time they left New York until they finally touched shore in Durban, South Africa.

Chapter 4

South Africa
1916-1919

The welcome Ralph and Ethel received from the missionaries in Durban was joyous and enthusiastic. It was also perplexing. Each missionary was certain that Ralph had come to help him in his particular area of ministry. Rather than become personally involved in the matter, Ralph wisely remained neutral, waiting for his official appointment at the Annual Missionary Conference in April.

To Ralph's dismay, he was appointed director of Edwaleni Training School. Teaching was not his field. Ralph had gone to Africa fully expecting to do pioneer evangelism, his special calling, and what he was trained to do. The missionary secretary had not thought to warn him he might have to do other things. With a keen sense of disappointment, Ralph went to Edwaleni.

Edwaleni, meaning, "on the rock," is a wild and beautiful rocky hill rising sharply from the Umtamvuna River on the border of Natal and Pondoland. Begun in 1906 by the Reverend N. B. Ghormley, the strategic location of the school made it accessible to both the Zulus of Natal and the Pondos in Pondoland. The steep, winding dirt road, which leads to the mission buildings on top of the hill, is still a challenge today. It must have been akin to daring adventure when Ralph and Ethel made their first ascent by ox wagon in 1916.

At the time they arrived, Edwaleni was fifteen years

old and had a small high school, a Bible training program, and an industrial department with about forty-five boys enrolled in a two-year course in carpentry, blacksmithing, and wagon making. The fact that Ralph longed to be doing another kind of work did not prevent him from assuming his school responsibilities with all the energy and skill he possessed. However, in his forthright manner, he wrote to the missionary secretary expressing his desire to be changed to evangelistic work just as soon as possible. Then he added:

> God has wonderfully helped us get ahold of things and by His help, have everything pretty well straightened out now.

The Pondo and Zulu tribes living around Edwaleni were a remarkably primitive and superstitious people who had had little contact with the white man or the gospel. Ralph and Ethel were eager to know them and took every opportunity to visit in their villages. In the following happy letter, Ethel describes her first visit to an African kraal.

> ... The kraal was two and a half or three miles from the house, so I decided to go donkey back.... My donkey was not used to having someone on his back, and at first thought he would rather not go to meeting, but by one leading him, and one behind urging him on, I finally persuaded him to go.... Right at an unexpected moment, when my feet were both out of the stirrups, my donkey began to kick and jump; of course I lost my equilibrium and found myself on the ground.... I was none the worse, with the exception of a dirty blouse, so I mounted again and started on. After riding some distance further, we came to ... a large kraal of six to eight huts....
>
> As this was my first visit, I hardly knew where to go or how to act. The hut in which the meeting was to be held had been specially prepared for us. The floor

had been well swept and the ashes removed from the fireplace.... The only member of our congregation that was present was a calf, which was tied to a stick by the wall and acted as though it was his regular abiding place.

... The walls were adorned with soot and were decorated with kettles, hoes, sickles, and their beds, which are hung up during the day and consist of a blanket and a mat.... Just over the calf's head there were hanging by a string, two or three tin spoons, just low enough so he could touch them.

The hostess was very polite to us and offered me a mat to unroll and sit upon; and the men, a couple of blocks of wood.... The boy who came with us had his Sunday school chart and talked a little while from it. They were very much interested in the picture. One of the other boys was prepared to preach.... The missionaries also said a few words.

Once during the meeting, we heard a commotion outside the hut which sounded as though the dogs were after the chickens. Of course our meeting had to stop until they could see what was the matter. They came back and sat down as if nothing had happened.

... How much was accomplished at that meeting, time and eternity will tell. One woman said she was soon going to repent. After shaking hands, we prepared to leave. The natives sized up the new missionaries and said, "They are just *izingani,*" which means "infants." I'm glad I still look young....

During his three years at Edwaleni, Ralph periodically reminded the Board that God had called him to do pioneer evangelism. He wrote:

... It would be very discouraging to me if I thought I had to remain in school work until my furlough is due. When I came here, I knew it meant to sacrifice getting the Zulu language because all of the boys here are compelled to talk English; and consequently, I do not hear it much, nor do I have to use it, which is so important in the learning of it. I have to shut my eyes to these things or I would get discouraged....

The responses Ralph received must have brought him small comfort. Once they cited an example of another missionary who found herself in a similar situation and had to remain there for twenty years because she was the one best fitted for the job. Even that did not shake Ralph's faith in what God had in store for him, and he found ways to promote the spirit of evangelism among his students.

... The spirit of the Lord has worked among the boys this past year. A few of the new boys have been saved and others strengthened....

In November, 1918, news of the Armistice brought joy around the world and reached even to the remote hilltop school at Edwaleni.

... About nine o'clock one morning, during the revival with Mr. Haley, a letter came from Dr. Backenstoe saying the Armistice had been signed; and I need not tell you that there was no more school that day. We hoisted the flags at the school ... and when I told the boys, they stampeded out doors and how they did shout and jump. I bought a goat for them, but the day was so full, they did not find time to eat it until about ten that night.... Just after the meeting we had a large bonfire on the edge of the hill near the schoolhouse; and thus ended the great, worldwide day of celebration at Edwaleni, and I think we did our part....

Each year the Free Methodist missionaries from Transvaal, Natal, and Portuguese East Africa meet together to transact mission business and find personal renewal in times of fellowship and worship. At their Annual Conference in 1919, one of the major problems facing them was the shortage of personnel in Inhambane, Portuguese East Africa. That part of the world, with its dense population and its hot, humid, unfriendly climate, had earned the reputation of being the white man's grave.

From the beginning of the mission, in 1885, when twenty-one-year-old G. Harry Agnew and the Reverend and Mrs. W. W. Kelley arrived in Inhambane, illness, death, loneliness, a shortage of personnel and funds, and an exceedingly difficult climate had plagued their valiant efforts to survive. The Kelleys had been forced to leave Africa, broken in health, within a year of their arrival. The Lincolns, who joined Agnew in 1888, were both dead from malarial fever within three months. In 1895, Agnew's bride of ten months, died of fever, leaving him alone once more, while he suffered repeated illnesses himself. Through the years, the Board sent others to Inhambane, but except for a few, they were able to stay only a short time, or else they relocated in other places. But Agnew's faith would not quit. Once he wrote in his journal:

> ... The town (Inhambane) is a perfect sink of moral corruption. I have often thought it would baffle Abraham, were he back on earth, to find five righteous people in that modern Sodom. Many times have I been around the town calling the people to repentance, many times wept and prayed over them, but as yet I have not seen even two inhabitants thereof whom I thought were ready to meet God. However, God must and will answer prayer, and I believe the day is coming when many, even there, will find Christ to the joy and satisfaction of their souls. ...

Harry Agnew died at the early age of thirty-nine, but his prophecy had come true. A church had been established in Inhambane; and the foundation, which he had laid at such cost, had slowly been built upon by those who followed. But now, due to various circumstances, only one lone missionary lady, Miss May Armstrong, was working in Inhambane as conference convened.

A few of the missionaries thought it would be wise to

close that field and concentrate their small resources in a more favorable area. Ralph and Ethel believed with others that God had a future for Portuguese East Africa; and furthermore, they believed God was calling them to be part of that future. In faith they requested a change of appointment to Portuguese East Africa. In the providence of God, their request was granted. That fall, Ralph and Ethel were joyfully on their way to Mabile mission station in the province of Inhambane, and their arrival marked a turning point toward advancement there rather than a mere holding on in desperation.

Chapter 5

Portuguese East Africa 1919-1938

Ralph and Ethel were happier at Mabile than they had ever been before. He wrote:

> ... I look back over the year and feel that I have accomplished so little, but the consciousness of having done the best I could is very sweet. I am especially grateful that this year finds me engaged in the work that I longed to be in since coming to Africa. I could not put my heart in the school work as I can into this Inhambane work which is my choice. ...

Again Ralph and Ethel began to acquaint themselves with a new environment. The languages, climate, and tribes were different in Inhambane from those in Natal. Eventually they would come to know all the tribes: the vaChopi near the Inharrime River, the vaTongas around Inhambane Bay, the vaTswas to the north and west, vanGuni by the Limpopo River, and the vaHlengwe to the far north and far west. But in the beginning, they tackled language study, and there were two languages to learn. Shitswa was the language of the vaTswa tribe (a branch of the vaHlengwe) with whom the mission worked primarily. Portuguese was the official language of the country in which all government business was conducted.

Ralph and Ethel were diligent and thorough as they studied. They learned not only to speak both languages but also to understand the language of the African's heart. This was essential if they were to effectively communicate the love of Jesus, and for them, sharing Jesus was the central purpose of their lives. Everything else they ever did, they evaluated on the basis of its relationship to that one main goal.

Of necessity, language study was pursued while on the job. In that do-it-yourself land, when a job needed doing, they had to do it. But God had prepared them well.

Ralph's love for farming, which he had willingly laid aside in obedience to God's call, was now an asset. In order to have food for their table, they had to keep cows and chickens, grow a large garden, and plant citrus trees. Ralph's skill as a hunter, which he had acquired as a lad, was needed to provide fresh meat not only for themselves, but for their African workers. His gun was their protection from poisonous snakes and the occasional lion, leopard, hippo, or elephant. Ralph's ability to plan with long-range vision was important in developing and guiding the young and growing church. His knowledge of building and mechanics was in almost constant use; and his ability to supervise and teach untrained laborers with patience, grace, and humor made it possible to rally cooperation, even on disagreeable jobs. Ralph's optimism and strong faith in God kept him going through it all.

Ethel was just as well suited for the responsibilities that crowded her days. She had a natural compassion for people which complemented her training in elementary missionary medicine; and even though she was not a registered nurse, she cared as best she could for the constant flow of sick who came to her door. Prepared medicines were scarce, but with a small apothecaries' scale she measured ingredients and mixed her own medicines according to simple recipes. Often, she used her own money to purchase the ingredients, and it was not unusual for her to go to the patient's home when he or she could not come to hers.

As a hostess, Ethel excelled, and her graciousness was appreciated by the guests she welcomed into their home.

Living as they did, so far from town, anyone passing through needed a meal, a bed, or both. Many passed through, and they all found her hospitality warm and genuine.

Fortunately, Ethel loved to sew. She had to make all her own clothes. Pretty cotton prints, especially floral pinks and blues, were her favorites. She had only two or three dress patterns, but she knew how to fit them perfectly and to vary them with bits of lace, ribbon, or buttons to prevent that look-alike appearance. She also taught the African women to sew for themselves and their families.

Ethel's spirit of adventure was a special boon on shopping days because the nearest town lay across Inhambane Bay. Those days began at dawn with a five-mile donkey ride to the Bay. There the plodding animals were exchanged for the creaking sailboat, an ancient, hand-hewn, wooden craft manned by a crew of husky Africans. No pier existed to facilitate boarding (nor has one ever been built), so passengers were obliged either to wade out through the quarter mile of shallow water to where the boat lay anchored, or be carried on the shoulder of a boatman. Being carried was preferred.

Once in town, shopping required hours of walking over hot pavement in order to cover the long list of purchases and business affairs. No one went to town unless the list was sufficiently long to warrant the journey. At the end of the day, there were many trips through the water to carry all the supplies to the boat. On the other side, supplies had to be carried ashore and tied onto the donkeys or given to carriers for the final five-mile jog home. Needless to say, that routine kept them from desiring the unnecessary things of life. But that was no hardship. Ralph and Ethel did not need extras to make them content.

Even with all of this, Ethel found time to plant flowers. She loved color and wanted their simple home to be bright and cheerful. A bouquet from her garden usually accented the plain white cloth on their dinner table.

Trekking took a large portion of Ralph's time, and Ethel always went with him. Ralph needed her companionship as well as her help. And besides, Ethel loved to go. She was particularly interested in the women and in the Sunday schools. As soon as she knew enough of the language, she helped to translate the International Sunday school lessons into Shitswa. These she taught to the pastors, who in turn taught them to the Sunday school teachers. Her goal of seeing a growing, active Sunday school on every outstation eventually became a reality.

Although visiting outstation churches brought Ralph and Ethel their greatest satisfaction, it was one of their heaviest responsibilities. In 1920, there were approximately forty-five evangelists and 1,102 members spreading over several hundred miles. The church had not yet produced ordained Africans to care for the work of serving Communion, baptizing, taking in members, and officiating at marriages. Such matters had to wait for the periodic visits of the missionary superintendent, who was required by the *Discipline* to visit every church at least once a quarter. One man was no longer able to visit so large an area that often — not when traveling meant riding a donkey or going by foot. The story of just one trip to a nearby district meeting will inspire appreciation of the situation, as told by Ethel.

... On Monday we started to prepare for going to district meeting ... a nearly three-hour donkey ride from the Mabile station. We ladies had to provide the food, dishes, cooking utensils, and bedding, while Bro. Jacobs got the tent in readiness.... Wednesday was beautiful and clear and it was a pleasure to start on our donkeys.

... Xereni is a Christian village and the houses are built in two rows which close together at one end. We pitched our tent on the sand near the center. It is made mosquito proof and has a floor of canvas attached to the walls so as to protect us from the sand flea. . . .

Wednesday afternoon and Thursday morning the evangelists arrived ready for business. Many of their people came with them, and each day others arrived, glad to meet each other. . . . This was the first general gathering held for nearly two years, owing to the epidemic of smallpox which has raged nearly sixteen months through Inhambane and is now raging in Chopiland. . . .

Between the many services Bro. Jacobs was continually hearing reports from the evangelists, revising the church roll, listening to seemingly endless matters, and writing the names of those who wished to be married or baptized, or who were ready to join the church. . . .

Mrs. Jacobs had brought medicine for the people and ointment for their sores. . . .

Thirty-three evangelists reported the work on their various charges and were relicensed. About twenty new evangelists were licensed, and new places are calling loudly for workers. Men offered themselves, but there is not money enough to send them, and there are not enough missionaries to rightly supervise the work. . . .

Saturday night at eleven o'clock, by the light of the lantern (because he could not find time to do it before), Bro. Jacobs married twenty-seven couples. It was a unique sight and resembled a ring meeting at our camp meetings at home. . . . The service was held out-of-doors under a large, spreading tree, and fifty-four men and women stood in a large circle around the missionaries, with the people behind. . . .

On Sunday, thirty-eight babies and sixty grown-ups were baptized. Sixty-five were taken into the church in full connection and 145 on probation. In the afternoon, three hundred or more knelt on the sand to receive Communion. . . .

For several years the mission had been searching for land to build a second station, so the district could be divided and supervised by two men. In 1921, a piece of property containing eight hundred twenty acres was purchased at a cost of $15,000. Inhamaxafo, as it was to be called, is located about sixty miles south of Mabile and fifteen miles from the Indian Ocean. Ralph and Ethel saw this as their opportunity to pioneer. Their fellow missionaries recognized that pioneering was their special calling and appointed them to the new station, with permission to go as soon as replacements arrived at Mabile.

A letter from Ethel provides a glimpse of their early days at the new station:

> After weeks of waiting, word came that the party of missionaries for Inhambane had reached Africa and would soon be there. Our hearts rejoiced, as this opened the way for some of us to begin the work on the new mission station. We hastily prepared to leave Mabile, one of the dearest spots on earth to me.
>
> Early one Monday morning, Miss Rice, Miss Armstrong, Mr. Jacobs, and myself started for our new place of labor.... The journey was long and tiresome.... About 6:30 that evening we arrived at Inharrime. Here we were met by the man from whom the land was purchased.... After loading the carriers with our tent, cots, bedding, bottles of drinking water, and a basket of provisions, we mounted our donkeys and started for our new place of abode. Our hearts bounded with joy as we rode along on the government road — with the moon shining down on us, making the night almost as clear as day.
>
> ... Early the following morning we chose a location for our tent, which we expected to be our only dwelling until we got possession of the house. Near to the tent was a nice large hut, which the man kindly offered to us; in these we settled. The hut served as a living

room, bedroom, office, and store room; the tent as a bedroom and dining room.

After a month or more, an outside room in the house was roofed and painted. But being roofed with grass and too flat, it leaked badly during a rain. During the first two weeks, two grass shelters were built providing sleeping quarters for our kitchen helpers. At the end of this time our goods arrived, bringing a stove. We were not long in getting it set up, as we were getting quite tired of eating smoked food as the result of cooking over open fires without pots made for that purpose. After much trouble, we got the stove up and we thought our trouble was at an end. But [we] soon found we had to plan our baking and ironing according to the wind.

Not having tables with us, every dry goods box, stump, and old piece of board was put into use. Our kitchen being small, it necessitated placing our table under a shade tree, where most of our work was done. This proved satisfactory during nice weather but was very trying and unpleasant when it rained. . . .

In order to live free from fever, one must have proper dwelling houses which are mosquito proof and built up off the ground, take quinine, keep out of the sun during the middle of the day, and keep dry. Living as we were compelled to, we were exposed to the sun, rain, and wind. We have appreciated the value of mosquito nets, helmets, raincoats and rubbers during these few months. Though exposed as we have been, we have had very little fever. God has been our shield night and day. Great are our privileges and possibilities.

God has given us a place where we are surrounded by heathen. Some are becoming interested and listen attentively as the Word of God is preached to them. Two have already chosen the Lord, and others are inquiring about the way and expressing their intention of leaving the ways of Satan and choosing the way which leads to heaven. Great is the darkness and strong is the enemy, but by faith in God we shall win the battle.

It is obvious from Ethel's letter that the matter of keeping healthy was a major concern, even though the danger of malaria had been greatly reduced with daily doses of quinine. Missionaries were still isolated. There was no doctor nearby in case of illness, and the graves of their predecessors constantly reminded them of their vulnerability. They trusted God to care for them, but they did not leave Providence entirely responsible for their health over the forty years they planned to work in Africa. Rather, they worked out a simple daily schedule which they believed would help them stretch their health over those forty years, and they followed it faithfully during their entire missionary career.

Each day they arose at dawn and worked hard while they worked. (Ralph said a person had not worked unless he had worked up a good sweat.) They took a short rest after lunch and quit their afternoon work when the sun went down. After supper they rested and chatted with friends, and if at home, they read, popped corn, or played a parlor game, then went to bed early. This plan not only worked well for them, but it also fit into the life-style of the Africans. Other missionaries who were wise enough and disciplined enough to follow their example reaped the same benefits.

Certain popular health theories abroad in those days had an additional influence on their lives. "Miasmic fogs" were believed to hover near the ground at night and cause illness. Because of that, Ralph designed his first Inhambane houses with two stories and built them on elevated sites so the missionaries could sleep above the fogs. Another theory warned against being wet or cold and especially advised against stomach chills. In response to that, they wore long-legged and long-sleeved woolen underwear and bound an extra red flannel cloth around their abdomens. Their heads were never to be exposed to the direct rays of the sun, so they wore thick cork helmets whenever outside during the heat of the day.

More significant than these precautions, of course, was the diligence with which Ralph and Ethel guarded their spiritual health. Ralph was always known to spend his first hour after dawn alone with God in prayer. He never neglected it. Ethel was just as consistent, but she waited until the early morning work was done, then called her two dogs, Blackie and Dicky, and walked down the hill to a certain tree where she prayed aloud while the dogs slept nearby.

A wise mission policy, aimed at protecting their health, was followed by all the missionaries. It provided that every other hot season, they should take a three-month rest in a cooler climate. Ralph and Ethel's turn for holiday came in January, 1921, shortly after they had moved to Inhamaxafo. It was difficult for them to go so soon, especially since it meant leaving Miss Latshaw and Miss Armstrong behind. Ralph was the only man on the station, and he felt responsible for their protection. But the ladies were not afraid.

The Jacobses had been gone only two weeks when the ladies were awakened one night by frantic cries for help. Arising quickly, they lit a lamp and hurried downstairs. There they found Pastor Stephani in a hammock, surrounded by his wife and the men who had carried him twenty miles to the mission.

A lion (found later to measure the length of a large ox wagon), had visited the pastor's village the night before and had taken a pig. In the morning, when they found the pig's remains, the men knew they would have to kill the lion before it returned to kill again. One man borrowed a gun, and the group set out to track the beast. They found it, shot, and missed. In the course of the pursuit, Pastor Stephani and two friends came upon the lion a short distance in front of them. They called the others to come with the gun, but before help could reach them, the lion leaped on Stephani, planting its powerful hind claws in Stephani's hips and its front paws on his chest. Stephani thrust his right hand into the lion's mouth, and with his left hand, he held its mouth so as to frustrate further attack. One friend valiantly grabbed the lion's tail and tried to drag it off, but it would not let go until it had been fatally wounded in the head.

The men then removed part of the lion's teeth, burned them in the fire, ground them into powder, and sprinkled the powder into Stephani's wounds to cleanse them and stop the bleeding. A cloth purchased from a passing trader was used for bandages. In the cool of the evening, they carried Stephani to the mission for further treatment.

Miss Latshaw and Miss Armstrong were teachers, not nurses. But they prayed and did their best, working through the night with their own home medicines. It was not enough. The bleeding continued and infection set in. After forty-eight hours of intense suffering, Stephani died.

Ralph and Ethel returned from their holiday in South Africa refreshed and ready to work. Bits from their own pens during the next two years summarize best the daily projects, problems, joys, and concerns of pioneering at Inhamaxafo.

RALPH. April, 1921

... A new brick house is being built on an elevated site near the lake, to be used by the single ladies. We were fortunate in finding good brick clay near the lake, also stone and sand. Enough hardwood timber has already been cut from the place to make the doors and windows of the new house. It might interest you to know that all these boards were sawed by hand, one of the trees used being 4½ feet in diameter. A number of men worked several days to fell the tree, cutting it all with their little hand-made axes. ...

So far, this place seems to be healthful.... Near at hand there are well-watered garden plots where vegetables can be produced in the cool season. Without fresh vegetables, canned goods largely make up the bill of fare; and this, if continued long, is not conducive to good health. . . .

There are about two hundred native tenants on this place in midnight spiritual darkness. . . . When we first came here, the drunken shouts could be heard day and night. . . . Besides hard work in the cane fields, sugar cane beer is all the white man, thus far, has brought them. It is our business to give them life instead of death.

With the exception of a Catholic school for boys, several hours of travel from here, this is the only mission station with white workers in this territory. . . . The spiritual, physical, and educational needs of this section are staggering. These people respond to the Word of Life, and by the help of God will we not say they shall hear?

More than one hundred miles of waterways are open before us, leading into Chopiland from this station. It is very probable that sometime in the future, a motor boat will be used to great advantage in carrying the gospel. . . .

RALPH. August 3, 1921

. . . I hope to have the house covered and in good shape for the hot season unless there is undue amount of delay in getting materials. I have just been held up for two weeks waiting for cement from Lourenço Marques. As I have been unable to purchase oxen yet, we have to break up the barrels of cement into loads. About forty carriers bring in five barrels at a trip. I expect to place the upstairs floor joists next week.

ETHEL. February 24, 1922

. . . Another hot season is nearly past. . . . We have stood the heat very well . . . but about a week ago it seemed as if we could not endure much more and keep going. We have had no rains to speak of this summer.... The gardens have been burned until they look as if it was winter instead of rainy season. The people are facing the winter with no food and no money to buy it. The men work about three months or more for a large sack of corn. Mr. Jacobs is now paying them more than they can get other places, so instead of raising their wages, we will have to give them a meal a day. It hurts me to see big men going to work in the morning carrying a native watermelon, a coconut, or a couple of ears of corn for their food during the day. Many times after working hard all day, they go home and to bed without anything more to eat. This is the second year that their gardens have been a failure and they are feeling discouraged....

We praise God for giving us this place among the people. He has given us their confidence, and I believe that in time many will turn from their sins to serve the true God. Some have already chosen the Lord and we have many things to encourage us.

There are such great opportunities here for a doctor or even a nurse. I count it a privilege to give out the most simple remedies, as by so doing, I come in touch with the people and have a chance to talk and pray with them. People come from miles away to get medicine.... How we would rejoice if a doctor and his wife could come out and take charge of the work while we are on furlough. I am sure he would be kept busy with just the medical work....

RALPH. April, 1922

... I came back last week from a trip of ten days to our stations along the Inharrime River. I started here in a boat, which I made last hot season. I visited a station a day. It was a great improvement over traveling by donkey. About twenty of the thirty stations of this circuit can be visited by water. I long for the time when I can give all my attention to evangelistic work.

RALPH. October 3, 1922

... The famine is carrying off the people by scores. This month and next will be the worst. I am trying to carry the people on the mission through, but some have died. I am feeding about seventy-five one meal a day and providing work for as many as possible. This morning I gave out a small tin of corn for seed to about one hundred twenty-five families. We have helped the evangelists and mission children and may have to do more....

ETHEL. April, 1923

... Two years and more have passed since the gospel has been preached at Inhamaxafo.... The leaven is working and there are already some visible results. A large place in the bush has been cleared and a Christian village built; also a small chapel where daily services are held. A Sunday school of an average of thirty-five scholars has been organized.... Instead of the sound of big drums which called the people to the dance and beer, the big chapel bell sends forth a call to all to serve their Lord....

As the people emerge from their darkness, a natural desire for knowledge is awakened. Many are asking to be taught.... It is touching to see middle-aged men beginning with the primer to learn, and with a slate and pencil, trying to write their names.... Many who once resorted to the witch doctors now come to the missionaries.... Along with the awakening come demands. The gospel must be given. The people must be taught. Their bodies must be cared for. This cannot be done without workers....

MAE ARMSTRONG. June, 1923

... Up to the present time, the erection of the buildings has consumed the energies of Mr. Jacobs until there has been little strength left for the supervision of the vast field assigned him. Two houses are now ready for occupants.... A temporary chapel is in place; also a two-room storehouse has been erected. Now a fitting chapel of a more permanent character is needed. The new station is also the home of the girls' school. . . . Now a building is needed to properly house these girls. . . . The calls of the sick and dying are heard on every hand. . . . We rejoice in the recent arrival of a nurse, Ruth Moreland, who has already begun her work. . . .

Of necessity, the gospel news must be proclaimed largely by the native evangelists. They have felt the call and are heeding it to the best of their ability, but their knowledge of God's Word is so limited that instruction must be given them if their work is to count. . . . "Oh," they say, "Why does someone not come to teach us? We are only like the donkeys. We know nothing." To hear them plead . . . and to have no workers who can be freed from other responsibilities sufficiently to shoulder this burden makes one cry out, "Oh, that the church might hear and heed their cry for help!"

At the end of seven years, Ralph and Ethel's first furlough came due. To them, furloughs were a necessary interlude, not to be prolonged. Civilization was hard on their nerves. They planned this furlough as they planned each one thereafter: to travel by freighter, so as to use as little of the Board's money as possible, to rest and visit their families, and to escape the public eye.

Ralph was uncomfortable before a crowd of white faces. He was small — five foot, four and three-fourths inches — and weighed one hundred twenty-five pounds. His quiet, reserved manner did not make him a popular deputation speaker. Someone described him while they were home, as being "compact in body, compact in prayer, sermon, and speech." Few American congregations had the opportunity to discover his greatness. Few people ever knew that in front of an African congregation he came alive and preached with ease and grace, enriching his sermons with homespun illustrations drawn from African life, which moved his audience to respond. Nor did many discover that his sense of humor was refreshing, his repertoire of stories delightful, and his store of knowledge remarkable.

Before furlough was over, he was restless. "We must get back to Africa. There's work to be done," he said. So they scheduled an early return to the field.

* * * * * * * * * *

During the 1920s, electricity and improved methods of transportation were making their entrance into Inhambane. In his typically brief style, Ralph recorded the following facts in his diary. (Ralph's diary, a tiny book, three by four inches in size, contains only thirty pages and covers the enormous span of fourteen years, from 1925-1939.)

February 17, 1926
Started electric light again (on battery).

September 2, 1926
Left for Delagoa Bay to buy first mission car.

September 9, 1926
Returned from Delagoa Bay with Essex car.

December, 1929
Traded old car for new Essex at Lourenço Marques and drove it to Natal. Arkseys rode with us as far as Johannesburg.

Other missionaries were more generous with their words and sent home vivid reports about these modern wonders and the effect they were having on the mission program. The Reverend Jules Ryff was amazed by what he saw when he revisited Inhambane in 1925 after an absence of eight years. He wrote:

... We were very pleasantly surprised to note the improved condition of the roads, which will now make it possible for the missionaries to travel hundreds of miles by car instead of by donkey as they have hitherto had to do. And who can estimate the value of this improvement to the missionary?... Think of the time saved, the exposure to the heat which donkey-riding imposes, and the night marches in malarial districts dispensed with.... A motor car may seem an expensive commodity, but it will save missions and missionaries much more than its value in time, health, and in prolonged service on the field....

Being made of pounded clay, these roads cannot stand heavy traffic, so carts and wagons, and even mules are not permitted thereon.

Another striking improvement is the installation of electric lights. The lights along the quay and the pier looked modern, but when I followed them in the native portion of the town, the mixture of civilization and heathen life was very contrasting.

Nothing material, however, shows as marked a contrast as the difference in the spiritual conditions of the native people, and the advance of the gospel. Our station at Inhamaxafo is a soul-cheering spot.... This station marks quite an advance in the physical aspects of our mission work in Portuguese East Africa. It points to better days, at least, compared with the equipment earlier times provided for our pioneers....

Mrs. Matilda Haley recorded the perils and pleasures of the automobile in evangelistic work:

... Early last week the two men of Mabile made another trip into the north country, Hlengweland. They got all the information obtainable about the condition of the roads, which left much to be desired. It really took faith in their cause to start out, with a prospect of twenty-five miles of sandy road at the last end, where they would have to go in second all the way, and neither water nor gasoline obtainable. So they loaded up with sixteen gallons of each, besides a large demijohn of boiled water for drinking, as well as blankets and food. We did earnestly pray that the Lord would perform a miracle with the car and get them through. We pictured them stuck in the sand, treed by lions or a passing herd of elephants who would play ball with the car, or attacked by leopards. But we took none of these things seriously, though they were possible. . . .

Upon the return of our heroes, we asked them if the lions were chained. Like two disappointed boys, they said they had not seen any lions, leopards or elephants, and not even the sandy road, for the Portuguese have built that last twenty-five miles of road, and the missionaries were the first to drive over it. . . .

They returned on Thursday noon, and on Friday morning we started for a quarterly meeting in Pandi, forty-eight miles in the opposite direction. I accompanied this expedition. We picked up our ordained native man, David, on the way, to show us the road. As we sped along, he said that the motor was a wonderful preacher — yesterday in Hlengweland and today in Pandi. . . .

As welcome and wonderful as they were, these mechanical marvels were also additional pieces of equipment for missionaries to keep in running order. Ralph accepted his mechanical friends with the same sense of stewardship that governed the rest of his life and possessions. They belonged to the Lord, and it was his responsibility to care for them as a worthy servant. In fact, he earned one of his few African nicknames "Kubinza" by the careful manner in which he guarded his automobile.

Any missionary can tell you that overloading is probably the chief cause of ill health among mission vehicles. No matter where or when the mission car travels, there are more than enough passengers, with baggage, asking to go along. The African version of the old adage seems to be: "Where there's a wheel, there's a way." Ralph solved the problem for himself by keeping his eye on the springs while the car was being loaded, checking after each addition, to make sure the weight was distributed evenly. When the car was weighted down just enough, he would raise his hand and declare firmly, *"Kubinza,"* meaning, "It's heavy." No more could be added, and the Africans knew that in his quiet and gentle way, Ralph meant what he said.

Flat tires were an unavoidable nuisance when rubber was thin and roads were abominable. However, when Ralph discovered that thorns in the elephants' diet were causing many of the punctures and that the number of flats could be reduced simply by driving around the elephant dung rather than running through it, the pleasure of travel increased considerably.

Ralph always watched his speedometer, and even when roads and vehicles were much improved, he never drove faster than forty to forty-five miles an hour — except when stampeding elephants made speeding essential.

Ralph was just as particular about changing the oil every thousand miles. To do that, he carried a supply with him and stopped beside the road, no matter where he was when the speedometer turned up the next thousand. There he would drain out the old oil, add new, and be on his way. When it came time to buy a new car, Ralph had no trouble selling the old one. His cars were known to be "a good buy."

The old methods of transportation did not disappear immediately with the advent of the automobile. The bicycle, the donkey, the boat, and the feet were still necessary. Missionaries still had to go where there were no roads. Whenever possible, Ralph used the automobile to visit the outstations on his district; but many, particularly those in the south, could be reached only by bicycle, donkey, or motor boat. To Ralph and Ethel, this was not a problem. Being with the people was their greatest joy, no matter how they had to get there. Ralph wrote:

... Last year my wife and I, together with a native cook-boy, made a trip from Inhamaxafo Mission Station to our stations at the south. The first two days were spent in the mission's little motor boat ... staying the first night at a village situated on the shore of a beautiful lake; and the second night we arrived at the place where a quarterly meeting was to be held. ...

This southern water trip affords the greatest variety of beautiful scenery of any that I have taken in Inhambane country. After passing out of the mouth of the great Inharrime River, we crossed a great inland lake nearly ten miles long. From this lake the waters narrow to a deep channel, winding through the low hills which border the Indian Ocean, and opening every few miles into beautiful lakes fringed with tropical vegetation. ... At places where the channel is narrow, the natives have built bridges composed of poles and bark rope. These bridges start from each shore and end abruptly in mid-stream, leaving a space ten or twelve feet wide between the ends for the passage of boats. One or two strong, loose poles span this space and on these, the people who cross have to balance themselves.

When the natives heard our motor, we would see them run and pull desperately at these large poles to remove them so we could pass. On one of these bridges, three or four small black-skinned urchins, without even the regulation twenty-four ounces of clothing, mustered up courage enough to stand on the end of the bridge near the passageway to see the white man's toot-toot pass. They stood their ground until wife turned the camera on them. They didn't wait to ask whether the camera shot pictures or bullets, but they all with one accord made a wild dash for safety along the bridge to the shore; and one, thinking he was not making enough headway, plunged over the bridge into the water and hid himself among the reeds. ...

After holding the quarterly meeting, at which the

evangelists and people from ten villages gathered, I left my wife and started on a hard, two-day trip to our southernmost station and back. Gasoline costs about one dollar a gallon in this land, and as I had used nearly half of my supply, I decided to leave the boat behind. Men cheerfully gave me donkeys to ride, and women freely carried my bed and box. I changed donkeys at midday, and about sundown reached the last station. . . .

How glad the people were to see me! I was shown to one of the best huts in the village . . . a nice large hut with freshly mudded floor. . . . I made my cot and lay down. Hearing the familiar ticking of a clock, I looked around, and there, hung on a real nail in the earth wall, was an alarm clock purring away as though it had always lived there. Someone had brought it from the gold mines in the Transvaal. . . .

Some of the young men of the village cooked me a fine supper — two kinds of porridge with peanut gravy and fried chicken. . . .

As they had not yet built a church in the village, evening prayers were held in the center of the village under the Southern Cross. There we sang and prayed together, worshiping Him who saves all who come unto Him. The missionary read John 3 and spoke briefly. . . .

The next morning we rode out of the village shortly after daybreak and on to other villages and other meetings. . . . Such is trekking in Inhambane. These people get into our hearts; we give them our best and they, in return, give their best. I was greatly encouraged on this trip by the evidences of a deepening of spiritual life among the people. . . . Those who have been praying especially for Inhambane had better stop a bit and praise the Lord and then go at it again.

Indeed, there was cause for praise. As Ralph expressed it:

Nothing short of God's marvelous power could keep those far-flung battle lines intact and moving forward.

One Sunday morning, while Ralph was preaching at Inhamaxafo, a witch doctor knelt at the altar, with her whole outfit of charms, and accepted the Lord.

Another encouraging event was the arrival of the Reverend and Mrs. Laurence Arksey, who were opening the long-awaited Bible school at Inhamaxafo. Ralph was grateful for these and other answers to prayer. Yet his pioneer heart was burdened for the baHlengwe people beyond the reach of the mission, who had never heard the gospel.

These baHlengwe had once been centralized in Portuguese East Africa, but tribal wars had broken them into subdivisions and scattered them as they fled, seeking safety from their enemies. Now, going west from Massinga, two hundred miles across Portuguese East Africa, and on into Rhodesia for another hundred miles, these people spread north and south between the Sabi and Limpopo Rivers. It was only natural that as the Free Methodist mission among the baHlengwe expanded, it would follow them up north and to the west into Southern Rhodesia.

Rarely could Ralph visit these distant places himself. His time was still filled with building up Inhamaxafo and superintending the schools and churches on his district. But around 1925, he had begun to send African volunteers on what he called "spying-out" missions into the north and west to preach and bring back reports of what they had seen and learned. These dedicated Africans were returning with burning hearts and stories of finding people who were living in deep spiritual darkness but who were receptive to the good news. As the African church members heard their reports, they were becoming inspired with a missionary vision of their own.

To the north, in a dry and difficult section called the Vilanculos Circumscription, were thousands of baHlengwe people, living without the gospel. Converts had been won there during the visits of these African volunteer evangelists, and they had formed into small groups of believers, but they were without a regular shepherd. The missionaries realized that a third station was needed north of Mabile to care for these new sheep. In 1927, plans were formulated to enter Vilanculos, and the Mission Board was asked to send two missionary couples and money to purchase land and build buildings. But the Board did not have the resources, and plans were laid aside.

At the close of 1928, Ralph sent Samueli, a native evangelist, on a second long trek west. Samueli returned with the letter from Chief Sengwe requesting missionaries to come over into Southern Rhodesia. This served to increase Ralph's sense of urgency to expand into the far west. But lack of funds and personnel prevented this move as well.

In America, depression was bringing hard times. Mission giving had dropped off, and for several years funds were not adequate to maintain the status quo. We cannot know the burden of prayer and concern that was carried by the members of the Mission Board during those years. But Ralph did not lose heart. In a letter to the missionary secretary, he expressed his faith that God would make it possible to advance and that he felt it would be soon. Then Ralph stated again that his call was to establish a church and pass on to new fields, and he felt that it was about time for him and Ethel to be moving on.

Opportunity to expand into northern Hlengweland came soon. More than thirteen thousand acres, situated sixty miles north of Mabile, were unexpectedly offered for sale at the amazingly low price of approximately sixty-five cents per acre. The location was ideal. There was a motor road beside the property, and there was building stone — an unheard-of thing in that sandy land for many miles around. Still, the cost was too great for such difficult times.

News of this offer reached America while missionary Nellie Reed was on furlough. When she heard of it, she requested permission to raise the money by "selling" land to individuals in America at sixty-five cents per acre. The Board recognized this as an inspired plan. The WMS sponsored her project, and Nellie went into action. She drew a map of the property, dividing it into acres, and for two years she traveled throughout the United States, "selling acres." Even the Junior Missionary Society members were excited about "owning land" in Africa. At least thirty-five hundred people in thirteen conferences participated — until every acre was sold. The purchase of this new property, which was called Massinga Station, marked an important advance in Portuguese East Africa. Ralph saw it as only the beginning.

> This year we hope to start the development of the new Massinga station, but we must still plant two other mission stations beyond.... For years, appeals have been made for missionaries ... nearly two hundred miles north of our Massinga station. Cries from Macedonia, and still we wait! Friends, I am persuaded that God has great work for our church here....

The South Africa Missionary Conference of 1930 was long to be remembered as the "Macedonia Conference." Crowds were so large that services had to be held outside under the cashew trees. Hundreds of people slept out in the open around camp fires at night for lack of sufficient shelters. Delegates from far and near came to report "sturdy strength and steady growth." Men from distant Hlengweland walked a full week to attend. From the first song until the end, the theme seemed to be "Awake, and go forth!" Reports showed that membership had reached 2,815, and the territory covered had stretched to thirty thousand square miles.

But progress had not been without price. The anti-Protestant government had imprisoned about one hundred men for preaching the gospel. Seven of the evangelists, who had gone into the new Hlengweland district, had been deported without trial and held in forced labor for a year. In his diary that year, Ralph had recorded that Nason and Charley were beaten, Sam's land was intruded on, Alfen was imprisoned, and Saul Mafumisa was exiled to Vilanculos for three years. But all these men were holding true.

The climax of the conference came during the missionary rally when an immense crowd listened spellbound to newly ordained Sam Gudo tell about the needs of their brothers and sisters to the north and west where he had visited recently. Testimonies were given by some of the "firstfruits" of that new work, and the audience rejoiced. A group of evangelists answered the call of God and were set apart to evangelize new areas. Ralph Jacobs and Jules Ryff were elected by the missionaries as a committee of two to explore the portion of Southern Rhodesia where the vaHlengwe tribe lives.

On August 18, 1930, the two men started from the Transvaal on what was for them, a joyful journey into unknown territory. They entered Southern Rhodesia at Beit Bridge, crossing the beautiful, wide Limpopo River, about which Kipling wrote so vividly; and for six days they traveled through the southeast section of the country as roads permitted.

The two-million black population of Southern Rhodesia lives on large tracts of land which have been set aside as Native Reserves. Europeans are not allowed to own land in these reserves except for those whose business compels them to, such as traders and missionaries. Native commissioners are appointed to handle governmental affairs in these reserves, and local chiefs are responsible for native affairs.

Numerous tribes inhabit Rhodesia, but the Shangaan tribe, which is a branch of the vaHlengwe, and the one in which our mission was interested, lives chiefly in two native reserves known as Matibi No. 1 and Matibi No. 2. These reserves form a quadrangle measuring one hundred miles each side. The government reports showed, at that time, at least ten thousand people living there with no religious work being done among them.

The Shangaans were concentrated north and south of the Lundi River, especially near the Portuguese Border; and as Ralph and Jules talked with them along the roads and in their villages, they responded with surprise and pleasure to hear white men speaking their language. To the missionaries, it seemed that opportunities for spreading the gospel were limitless.

Ralph had hoped to reach Chief Sengwe's kraal in Matibi No. 2 Reserve, but lack of roads forced them to stop short of that goal. However, the government officials with whom they spoke were helpful and encouraged them to establish Free Methodist schools, churches, and hospitals.

In their report to W. B. Olmstead, the missionary secretary, Ralph and Jules detailed their findings and estimated that a new mission could be started in Southern Rhodesia with no more than two thousand pounds. Then they said:

> We desire that this small voice calling us to occupy will be heard by our home church. If we listen and respond, God himself will open the way. . . .

The Mission Board listened. They were interested. But the continuing depression made it impossible to begin such a venture. The missionaries were disappointed but not disheartened. They knew that in His time, God would make it possible. Ralph and Ethel were almost due for their second furlough, and they anticipated "breaking new ground" during their next term.

* * * * * * * * *

The Jacobses did, in fact, return from furlough just in time to "break new ground" at Massinga. It had taken that long, as well as much patience and grace, to work through the miles of red tape necessary to obtain government permits for building and carrying on evangelistic work in that new district. But permission had finally been granted. The missionary staff had not increased to cover this extra station, so Ralph was asked to assist the Reverend A. E. Haley at Massinga, in addition to his regular appointment as superintendent of Inhamaxafo.

Immediately following conference, the two couples prepared to camp at Massinga for two and a half months while the preliminary work was accomplished. With good humor, Mrs. Haley described their first strenuous days.

... When preparing for camp life for that period of time ... my favorite portion of scripture is: "They shall go no more out forever."

It was past noon when we drew up by the side of the road. ... At last, here we were — a party of four missionaries and five native helpers, in a touring car and a truck; and we had arrived about two hours after noon on the same day we started. ...

The men had gone to a little native village and inquired if we were not near an old road. ... Yes, we were right at that road. A young man would come and show the way and help clear the growth of bushes and grass. ... Within a few yards we had crossed the border into our acres, and within an eighth of a mile we came upon a small grassy knoll and camped. Such an unloading as we had!

The men had to go at once with a truck and several empty gasoline tins to a well some distance away (and over a very bad road) for a supply of water, while the women tried to get things in order, amid one contingent after another of visitors, wanting to see everything, but giving us a very hearty welcome. A gift of a fowl was brought that night. A day or two later the chief honored us with a visit and a gift of a fowl. Next day was Saturday and we got our camp well set in order and never welcomed the day of rest more, for we were weary!

At first, Ralph and Mr. Haley were mystified by the Africans' refusal to work for them. Then they discovered that the site they had chosen was the burial ground of former chiefs. When they moved to another location, the Africans willingly joined the crew, and everyone worked hard. But even so, it was an enormous undertaking.

... We have literally had to dig ourselves in; and that, in the heavy bush. At present, we have gathered a gang of workers ... and have built one native hut, which one family occupied, and are building a second one for the other family; for it is far too hot now to live in tents. We have two small V-shaped huts for our native help, a thatched roof with open sides for a dining room, a small wattle and daub place for a storeroom, and an extended roof made of old iron for a garage.

We are on the edge of a very thick jungle, hence it is very hot, and the soft sand makes it very tiring. We hope a little later to have our dining room and paths hardened by a sandy clay, obtainable by digging a few feet. When moistened and pounded, this is quite an improvement.

This is a waterless country, many women taking two days to make the round trip for water. We are drilling and are down about 78 feet.... Indications are good, and we hope soon to report success....

Earnest prayer had gone into the choosing of a drilling site, and earnest prayer accompanied their daily labor. With unusual detail, Ralph chronicled their progress in his diary.

September 1, 1932
   Finished digging well to rock (48 feet) with posthole digger on ½-inch pipe.

September 6, 1932
   Put tools in hole and finished preparations to drill with spring pole. God has helped us mightily.

September 7, 1932
  Commenced drilling in the rock.

September 16, 1932
  Noon: The bailer came up dry. A fissure had drained away the bailings.

September 17, 1932
  Now 30 feet into rock of a whitish color limestone. Tailings like whitewash; 78 feet deep.

September 20, 1932
  Came back to Inhamaxafo for District Meeting and found a lion had been within a few hundred yards of our house and killed a pig.

October 15, 1932
  Struck water at 1:05 P.M. Praise God who is faithful and true! The chief and others had called at times while we were drilling and said that there was no water in the country and in this bush, and also we would fail because we hadn't *pahlela'd* (sacrificed) to their gods.

Ralph said he had never been so conscious of God back of them, pushing them on, as while digging that well:

He helped us over every difficulty, and there were many. But as we arose, one after another, a way was opened until the final victory was secured.

The Africans, true to their belief, refused to use the water until they had sacrificed to their water god and until the witch doctor had pronounced the water "good." After that, they used it gladly, walking long distances and carrying away as much as they were able.

Over the next six years, Ralph and Ethel were constantly on the move from Inhamaxafo to Massinga, and the missionary's usual quota of unusual happenings followed them. A few were recorded in Ralph's diary.

September 18, 1933
  Finished setting out 1,200 eucalyptus trees in

Pennsylvania Avenue, Inhamaxafo; 100 more to set out later so as to finish lining the whole road on both sides.

October 31, 1933

Locusts came from the west and left that evening, going around our mission. God spared us this plague.

November 1, 1933

At 9 A.M. some locusts came across the lake and up to the edge of our river gardens, but were driven back by people beating pans, by fire, and north wind.

August 1-14, 1934

Built church at Massinga. There was an eclipse of the sun while I was working on the roof.

February 27, 1935

Evangelists convention at Magula. I had boils in my arm pit.

July 1, 1935

Left for Hlengweland West with Arksey and Sam Gudu and Haley. Took the Massinga truck. We were gone 5 days; 225 miles.... Took 5 cases of gas for whole trip.

October 8, 1935

Sam Gudu dreamed a week or two past that he was in Hlengweland in a thicket of thorns. Many people passing along outside. He tried to get out to them to tell them of Jesus, but the long thorns held him in. He preached until his voice gave out. He awoke, then slept and dreamed again. He was still held in the thicket by the great Hlengweland thorns, but he preached to the people passing on the outside of the thicket. He saw a great open road passing by the thicket and leading *north*. He awoke, then slept and dreamed the third time. He saw at the end of the great road leading north, a temple of the Lord and many people going into it. He asked me if he was foolish to believe this dream. I answered that I thought the dream came from God and was prophetic of events to come — the extension of God's work in Hlengweland.

November 1, 1935

What appeared to be a meteor was seen by the natives about sundown. It came from the west with a great light and sound — seemed to strike the earth somewhere in Cumbana area.

August 4, 1936

Sister Matilda Haley was operated on for cancer, in Durban, today.

August 18, 1936

A meeting of the missionaries was held at Inhamaxafo for the purpose of appointing someone to Massinga in Bro. and Sis. Haley's place. Ethel and I were appointed there.

August 22, 1936

Moved to Massinga.

November 7, 1937

Terrible hail storm at Massinga, about 5 P.M. Hail 1½ inch in diameter.

April 23-30, 1938

Fred Eicher, the Austrian hobo artist, stayed at Massinga.

May 19, 1938

A buffalo went through the garden at the front of our house in the night.

While lack of funds had prevented the opening of Southern Rhodesia during those years, the spirit of missionary fervor had grown stronger. In one respect, depression had been a blessing in disguise. When money from America grew scarce, the Africans were inspired to take the responsibility upon themselves to support their evangelists. Other encouraging signs of God's blessing were seen as well. The WMS, which Mrs. Haley and Ethel had organized, was blooming, and the women were taking their places in the church. Young men were continuing to dedicate themselves for evangelistic services. Two new missionary couples, Victor and Susan Macy and Wesley and Lela DeMille, had come to Portuguese East Africa in 1936 and 1937. Thirty new outstation churches had been opened, with a gain of 837 new members. The entire field had been pretty well surveyed by Ralph's "spying-out" parties. Several evangelists were located in the center of the tribe, supported by the African church. A church had been started near the border of Southern Rhodesia.

By 1937, the desire of the missionaries and of the African church to expand into Southern Rhodesia had reached such an intensity that it must surely have been communicated to the American church by Mr. Arksey's powerful call to action.

> ... We must, by nature of our calling, advance or die. Our policy here in Portuguese East Africa has been one of pressing forward into the regions beyond. We have been commissioned to take every accessible bit of territory.
>
> If we follow the Shangaan (baHlengwe) tribe, it naturally leads us to ... cross over the border into Southern Rhodesia.... We already have outposts up to the border.... Furthermore, we have sent scouts into Southern Rhodesia who have gotten in touch with several native chiefs, and we have approached the British authorities regarding permission to enter this country officially....
>
> There are young people at home in America and Canada who have already dedicated their lives for service in Africa. Souls are dying in darkness, crying for missionaries. What shall we do? Are we going to let this opportunity pass?
>
> We have been given permission by the missionary secretary to make a trip into this territory to investigate every possible phase of the situation ... but we have been distinctly told that no money can be forthcoming until after the next quadrennial meeting....
>
> Here is the situation: Land ahead to be possessed;

the army has volunteered, the orders have been issued, "Go, ye," and we must advance or die spiritually. Yet we are told that there are no supplies, no food for at least two years more. Who ever heard of an army advancing on food promised two years from now?

We want bully-beef! Someone has said that the missionaries should pray more about needs. Yes, we should pray more, but there are some good people who are hoarding the supplies. Unlock your cupboards and give us a few tins of beef and biscuits.

In the next war, they will probably put profiteers and hoarders in the front lines to be shot first. I'm not suggesting that anyone should be shot at sunrise, but I do pray that God will stir up your pure hearts to let us have enough rations so we can build a permanent fortress for Christ in Chief Sengwe's village in Southern Rhodesia.

Finally, at conference in 1938, the missionaries requested Ralph and Mr. Arksey to make a second trip into Southern Rhodesia, this time to apply for a mission site. Stirred by an eloquent appeal from their own evangelist, Jacobe Bande, the African church contributed the relatively large offering of $250 toward the opening of this new field.

Within a short time, the two men were in Southern Rhodesia, and again the government officials gave them every possible encouragement and help. However, the native commissioner, Mr. Ling, could not approve their request to establish the main mission station in Matibi No. 2 Reserve, near Chief Sengwe's kraal. That, he said, was in the low veld where malaria was a serious health hazard. Also, communications and securing supplies would be difficult because it was two hundred thirty-five miles from Fort Victoria, and much of the road was only a trail through the bush. Instead, Mr. Ling suggested that the mission be given both Matibi No. 1 and Matibi No. 2 Reserves for their mission work, and that the main station be located in Matibi No. 1, somewhere near the Lundi River.

For an entire morning Mr. Ling tramped through the bush with the two missionaries, looking for a spot that would be ideal for a mission station. Finally they found one, and Mr. Ling said, "Build here!" The men felt it was God's choice, and they made formal application for those one hundred acres on the south bank of the Lundi River.

That beautiful piece of land in the northern corner of the Reserve was only seventy miles from the small town of Fort Victoria, where supplies could be purchased, and was within one mile of the main road. There would always be an abundance of water on the property. It contained sufficient sand, gravel, and ant hills for building, and sufficient arable land for the development of a school. It was also rich in natural beauty.

Across the rocky, island-studded river could be seen endless green forests and giant, bare granite *koppies* (small rock mountains) rising five hundred feet into blue sky. During rainy season, the river would roar in torrents; and in dry season, large, deep pools would remain between the great boulders, providing homes for the sly crocodiles and grunting hippos. At night the occasional bark of the bush buck was heard. Mornings and evenings were announced by the soft chanting of mourning doves.

Besides that, Mr. Ling informed them that as soon as permission for the lease was granted (at a token fee of three pounds per year) they could make application for passes for native Portuguese evangelists to enter the country and begin preparing the way for proper, government-recognized schools. There would be financial grants to the mission schools and medical facilities as soon as they met government standards. It was Mr. Ling's personal belief that native development should be founded upon religious training, or else it would be useless. The church, he said, would be left free to do all the evangelical work it desired. Being a British colony, the official language of the country was English. Missionaries would have to learn only one foreign language — the language of the African tribe with whom they worked. Such favorable conditions were almost unbelievable to men who had struggled so long with difficult government regulations. Ralph and Mr. Arksey returned home to Portuguese East Africa full of faith. They sent their findings to the Board, recommending that Rhodesia be entered immediately.

The WMS in America was responding to the stirring reports about Southern Rhodesia by voting to give the Mission Board $2,000 to help open the door into Chief Sengwe's land. With that as a token of God's blessing upon the project, the missionary secretary, Harry F. Johnson, sent the following message to the field:

> Your committee recommends that we open work in Southern Rhodesia as soon as funds are available, and we hereby authorize the securing of a site this year. **We have a thousand dollars from the WMS general organization** on hand for the beginning of this project. It is to be known as the WMS project, and all things being equal, they expect to give us another thousand dollars a year from now for the establishment of the mission.

A few days later the Rhodesian government informed the missionaries that the proposed mission site had been granted to the Free Methodist Church, possession to be effective on January 1, 1939. As Ralph expressed it, only one thing was lacking — the *man*.

Ralph and Ethel were due furlough and had gone to Ebenezer Rest Home in Natal, South Africa, to make preparations for their voyage home. The last seven years of continuous, hard, physical labor had taken their toll. They were both weary and were anticipating a time of rest and renewal. However, the European situation looked threatening, and they did not wish to be traveling if war should break out. They were also considering the cost to the Board of their overseas voyage. As far as missionary personnel for opening Rhodesia was concerned, Ralph assessed the situation like this:

> ... Unless another couple is sent out, I can't see how we can spare either Brother Arksey or myself from down on the coast. If we wait to open the station until I return from furlough, it would only be about one year until Bro. Arksey's furlough is due. Without furloughs, we might be able to get along with three couples in P.E.A., but furloughs are indispensable. ...

Ralph and Ethel finally decided they should furlough in Cape Town, South Africa. Arrangements were completed and they were ready to leave when this letter from the Mission Board changed everything.

> How would you like to go to Rhodesia and start building the house on that site granted by the Rhodesian government, instead of coming home on furlough? I can think of no one more capable of doing that job of constructing a new mission station than *you*. You say in your letter that you have everything but the "man" necessary to go forward. Of course, I see there are some obstacles in the way of going forward immediately: for example, you have no mode of transportation, you have not sufficient funds, you are in need of a furlough, etc., etc. However, those things might come if we moved forward by faith.
>
> As for sending another couple to Portuguese East Africa, I think that day is a long ways off. Now we will have to do the best we can with what we have to do with.
>
> Please send me an airmail letter on what you think could be done under the present circumstances. ...

Ralph's response was not surprising:

> ... We had all plans made to go to Cape Town when your airmail letter came like a bolt out of the blue; but there was no confusion, only a calm assurance that this was the will of God for us. Where He leads, there we

will go by His grace and strength. Gladly do we turn our backs on the needed rest and face the battlefield again.... If we have to leave on furlough in a year's time, I don't see anyone to fill in after us, but I suppose we must leave that to faith. The whole work there in Rhodesia has thus far only opened as we go forward....

Ralph and Ethel had saved twenty-five pounds from their holiday allowance, and now they asked to use that money for the upkeep of their new car during the remainder of the year. Ralph went on to explain that he had purchased a new Chevrolet Road Cab for Rhodesia, so ... the problem of transportation, and other mountains, were disappearing. To the Board's puzzled query as to how he was able to buy a car, Ralph admitted that he had used the local church's two-hundred-fifty-pound offering for Rhodesia, his own personal tithe, and Christmas gift money from his mother.

Their three-month vacation at Natal had been a gracious and loving gift from God, who knew it would be seven more years before they could furlough in America.

Ralph and Ethel left for Rhodesia with only a bed and a few cooking utensils in the back of their pickup truck. They were willing to live under any conditions necessary in order to get the new mission started. The final entry in Ralph's diary appears to have been written hurriedly across the page:

March 25, 1939
   Arrived Southern Rhodesia.

That, however, was not the end; it was only the beginning of their third and most challenging pioneer venture of all!

The Vahlanganyete (WMS) on a witnessing trek.

Sengwe school in 1968.

Inhamaxafo mission home and single ladies' residence built by Ralph Jacobs.

Students earn their way through Bible school by working in the fields.

Ralph Jacobs on trek.

Typical Shangaan village scene near Sengwe.

A Malawi pawpaw tree.

A spirit hut in Hlengweland.

Lundi River near the mission, with koppie in the background.

Ralph Jacobs planted this avenue of eucalyptus.

Lundi water system in the early days.

Hospital outdoor waiting room at Nhaloi in 1973.

Clinic built by Mr. Jacobs. Patients come from many miles away.

Mr. Jacobs pays his workers.

Ralph and Ethel in their Chikombedzi home.

Chapter 6

Southern Rhodesia 1939-1955

According to Ralph, everything moved like well-oiled machinery on their trip north to Southern Rhodesia. At the border they did not have to pay a penny of duty on their new car. Within three days Ralph had seen the native commissioner, Mr. Ling, and things were in order to start building at once. That suited Ralph perfectly. If anything distressed his energetic, do-it-now spirit, it was delay.

Their first guest was Mr. Ling, who quickly warmed to their hospitality as he sat on a box and drank tea from an enamel cup. Ralph and Ethel needed and appreciated his friendship and advice. They had much to learn about this new land.

Ethel watched Ralph set to work with the same youthful energy he had possessed at Inhamaxafo years before, and she knew God was supplying strength for the day, just as He had promised.

Within two weeks, they were moved into two temporary huts. The walls were not mudded, but it was still warm in April. They did not mind the fresh air blowing in between the poles — at least not yet. Their bed was built up on sticks and over it hung a large mosquito net. A stick, stuck in the mud wall, served as a rack from which they hung their clothes. To add a homey touch, Ethel purchased a kitten from an African for eighteen cents. Puss, as Ethel named her, was a great deal of company — and later, her daughter, Fluffy, joined the family. A black-and-white terrier, Lady, was Ralph's outdoor companion.

But living was not all joy. Hot season brought heavy rains, which in turn brought hoards of malarial-bearing mosquitoes. The daily dose of quinine prevented fever, but it did not keep them from being badly bitten. By June, cold season was upon them, and their pole house left much to be desired. Cold wind blew in through the hanging reed door. A fire was built on the ground outside, and they sat around this, wrapped in blankets to keep warm. Ethel wrote during that time:

> ... Can you imagine me sitting by a fire? I am in our open dining room hut with a fire built on earth floor. The sun is covered and there is a cold wind. We will be able to move into one room of the house in a couple or three weeks now. What a happy day it will be! ... Oh, it is cold this morning!

At Mr. Ling's suggestion, a formal stone-laying ceremony for Lundi Mission was planned for June 8, 1939. Cars began to roll in two hours ahead of time, with government officials, police, traders, and ranchers. Every white person living in the area within fifty miles was there — thirteen in all! A load of chiefs and their Indunas (sub-chiefs) came in the commissioner's truck, and everyone was joyful that at last, missionaries had come to their country.

Mr. Ling addressed the crowd in fluent Shangaan, telling the Africans that if they obeyed the missionaries' words, they would be shown the Way of Life. His own work, he said, was secondary in importance to the work of the mission. Then, striking the cornerstone sharply with a trowel, he declared,

> I trust that this mission and its work will be as strong and solid as this stone.

Two or three chiefs were given opportunity to welcome

the missionaries, and Chief Sengwe was one of them. Other Africans from far off sections appealed for someone to teach in their areas too.

How, Ralph and Ethel wondered, could they possibly meet all the requests? So much building remained to be done before the mission would function properly, and the real and greater work was to teach the Word and help the people to grow. Never had they been more aware of the meaning of Jesus' statement, "The field is ripe unto harvest, but the laborers are few." Fervently they prayed the Lord of harvest to supply laborers. How marvelously that prayer was to be answered.

Materials and skilled labor costs in Rhodesia were about twice as much as they had been in Portuguese East Africa, so Ralph had sent a request to Mr. Arksey for one or two African volunteer masons to help him until Rhodesian Africans could be trained. They responded and came. Then Ralph realized that if he was to make the best use of the cool, dry season for building, he would need the second thousand dollars from the WMS before next October as promised. The Board did not have money to advance, but God supplied it through a donation from a Mrs. Leach in Rhode Island. This cleared away any lingering doubts the Board may have had concerning God's will for Rhodesia.

> ... We wish to be sure to follow the Lord in His guidance concerning this new mission field. When the WMS so generously gave their $1,000 last fall, and then a few months later a lady from Rhode Island sent us a thousand dollars for that project, it seemed to us that it was the Lord's will for us to go forward immediately, rather than wait longer. ...

As Ralph proceeded with courage and faith, God's blessing was poured out. From the beginning, the heathen men who were working on his building crew, responded to the Word Ralph preached each morning. Many expressed a desire to become Christians, and they wanted to buy

Testaments and songbooks. The first six books were sold immediately and more were asked for. In the mornings, Ralph would find the men around the campfire looking through their primers or hymnbooks, even though they could not read.

Sunday worship services, which were held under the large, shady trees near the river, were well attended. Curiosity brought the people at first, just to see and hear the little white man who dressed so neatly in khaki shirt, long khaki pants, and sun helmet. They stared, too, at his little, plump and smiling wife with the curly, graying hair. But their curiosity was soon replaced by the Holy Spirit's conviction, and for two years, rarely a Sunday went by without people "choosing the Lord." After a week of strenuous labor, Ralph and Ethel went to Sunday service tired in body; but they came away like giants, refreshed with new wine, from seeing the hunger of the people and young men choosing the Lord. By June there was an inquirers' class of seven members, most of whom were young men and heads of families.

September saw the completion of the first three rooms of the Jacobses' house, and they moved in with thanksgiving. At last Ethel had chairs for her guests to sit on. She admitted that she was beginning to feel ashamed to hunt for box chairs when government officials visited. Mr. Ling felt enough at home to bring his own camp bed when he needed to spend the night.

The Lundi church was also completed that month, and the dedication day dawned clear and bright with a hot sun rising over the koppies. Soon lines of people were coming from all directions. Women and girls walked in, dressed in their brightest Shangaan skirts and head scarves. Men and boys rode bicycles or came by foot. Again Mr. Ling brought other officials. The congregation was a unique and colorful assortment of people.

Following the message, Ralph took the first twenty-one converts into the church on probation. The offering that day amounted to $101, two live fowls, three eggs, a little grain, and six pawpaws. Afterwards, Ethel served dinner to all the white visitors, and tea was served to the Africans who had come from a distance. It was a day to remember!

From the very beginning, the church spread quickly beyond the Lundi area into other sections of the reserve. In response to calls from headmen and chiefs from near and far, meetings were held and many people repented. Mandumbu is one example of how those churches were born and grew.

In June, 1940, three strangers came to see Ralph — a tall, sober fellow, a young man, and a gray-haired old man. Ralph greeted his visitors and squatted on his house steps to listen while they told him their story.

They represented three groups of villages in the south that wanted to be taught the way of salvation. They also wanted schools for their children. Ralph could not arrange for three extra meetings, but together, they decided to hold a service fortnightly at Mandumbu, a central point about thirty-five miles south of Lundi that all could attend, and one Ralph could reach by car most of the time — if he drove carefully. The meeting place was a great, granite rock, perhaps half an acre in size, from which a large tree grew out of a cleft near one side. The tree provided shade for the audience, and the flat rock served as pews. A raised rock was the pulpit.

Rain, and confusion over the date, caused the first few meetings to fail, but then people came in crowds and God began to speak to them. Within a few months, men and women "chose the Lord," and a small body of believers was formed. It seemed that God had prepared their hearts to receive the message.

One man whom God apparently used in this preparation was Mboweni. As a child, Mboweni had gone with his father to the Transvaal. There he had been converted and trained in the Dutch Reformed church and schools. In 1895 he had been sent back to Rhodesia to minister to his own people, and in 1916 he had moved to a site only fifteen miles from Lundi where he had carried on his church work more or less alone. The work had not grown significantly, but because of his influence and faithfulness, the gospel was readily accepted in that area.

When Ralph went to Rhodesia, he knew he would soon be needing help to pastor new churches, so he wrote to Portuguese East Africa asking for volunteer African evangelists to minister in Rhodesia for a few years. Two young couples, who had been led of the Lord the year before to "lay themselves on the offering plate," responded immediately. The next year two more men and their families joined them; and later, two single men. When these pastors arrived, they found small groups of believers ready and waiting. One of the couples was sent to Mandumbu; and soon after, the people there joined together to erect a church, sixteen by forty feet, and a two-room house for the pastor. Sunday services were conducted each week, and four class meetings were held within a radius of six to eight miles. It reminded Ralph of God's promise, "In the wilderness shall waters break out, and streams in the desert" (Isaiah 35:6).

Another of these Portuguese East Africa pastors was sent into Matibi No. 2 Reserve to open a church at Sengwe's kraal, so that within six months from the time the Jacobses arrived in Rhodesia, the bell was being rung at Sengwe. The people there were hearing the Word preached regularly. However, visits from the missionary were few because of the difficulty of traveling those 180 miles.

Ethel wrote of one of their visits to Sengwe's kraal:

> This finds us at Sengwe's [kraal] where the bell is being rung. I am sitting now only a few yards from the big tree under which the bell is hung. We arrived Wednesday night after dark. . . .
>
> Chief Sengwe happened to be at the assistant commissioner's office as we were passing by. He is an old man, . . . lame from rheumatism, so a ride home in

the car looked better to him than a four-day ride on a donkey. A place was made for him in the car and we were soon off.

It was rather cloudy and just the right kind of morning to see wild animals, and we were not disappointed. The herds of zebra, wildebeest, giraffe, and antelope were beautiful in their wild setting. Just seeing these rewarded us for all the hard work it took to prepare for the trip.

Our road was mostly through thick bush, and in many places we saw fresh elephant spoor and trees that were broken over by them. ... It gave us a rather uncanny feeling, seeing all those traces of elephants and then driving fast around sharp curves in the road, never knowing what was around the turn. ...

In the afternoon we passed a transport driver's place and stopped and had a cup of tea with him. ... His words regarding the road further on were not reassuring. We pressed on, but the further we went, the less assured we were of making it through; and finally we came to a dry, sandy river bed which took us two more hours to work our way across. ... How grateful we were when we saw the car make its last hard pull up the bank which landed us on hard soil again!

The rest of the trip had to be made in the dark, and through country where the only road that could be seen was a footpath. ... The only reply we could get from Chief Sengwe when asked if this was the way was, "I don't know, as it is night." The car was then stopped and the old man would crawl out and go ahead and look for familiar trees or something that would give him a clue to where we were. Finally he returned and said he saw a fire far off. ... After awhile he called out and said when we came to two sticks by the side of the path, we were to turn off. ... The two sticks finally came into view. ... After a few more miles we were greeted by the light of a lantern and saw that it was the evangelist himself, coming to meet us. How happy these two faithful servants of Christ were to see their missionaries after being shut off here so long, away from friends, and in a strange land! We were too tired for more than a casual greeting and prayers that night.

This morning, while I was visiting with the evangelist's wife, she related the trials and hardships they have been through during the past year. Gardens planted had been destroyed by wild animals.... Sickness had laid her low for three months and nearly claimed her life, after which she gave birth to a little boy. ... The people were afraid to help her in time of need, thus leaving her to herself and their eleven-year-old daughter.... She said God helped her and did not forsake her.... Never once was there a hint of desire to give up and return to their home in Portuguese East Africa.

Chief Sengwe now hears the bell ring, but its message has not yet entered his heart; he has not yet reached the place where the uncompromising way has more attraction for him than his beer. However, we were happy to see other fruits of the ringing of the bell. There are a few in the inquirers' class, but as yet only one felt he was ready to be taken into the church on probation. He is a very promising young man and is already being used of God. ...

The saga of those consecrated African missionaries from Portuguese East Africa is a beautiful example of courage and dedication. They left behind all they possessed, and they risked danger and hardship to walk for two to three weeks across miles of wilderness just to reach their new home. In Rhodesia they were strangers, without any means of support until they could plant and harvest their first crop. That alone was a severe test for the African who has strong ties to his home and garden. Only God could have given them courage and strength for such an undertaking.

Ralph and Ethel felt personally responsible to provide their food until they could grow their own. But drought brought crop failure, and one year lengthened into several years. The financial burden on the Jacobses' limited salary was considerable before the men were finally self-supporting.

* * * * * * * * * *

At each place where a church was established, a kraal school for the beginning grades was also opened, and the church building served as the schoolhouse during the week. Results of the gospel and of education were quickly visible in those areas. The children, who had been illiterate and dirty a short time before, were wearing clean clothes and eagerly reading. Many were finding the Lord. A large percentage of those in the churches were under the age of twenty-one. The future looked bright for the Free Methodist Church in Southern Rhodesia.

The first six kraal schools spread 180 miles throughout the two reserves, from Lundi to Sengwe. Calls for new schools kept coming faster than Ralph could find suitable teachers. He was allowed to hire untrained teachers just to get the schools started, and those teachers demanded comparatively little salary, but neither did they qualify their schools for government grants. Ralph needed not only trained teachers; but he wanted trained teachers who were Christian and could lead the services on Sunday if there was no pastor.

Lundi Central School was to be a high school for the graduates of the kraal schools, but the first class at Lundi was made up of children of all ages who had never been to school before, and the teacher was untrained. A missionary teacher was urgently needed to guide the development of the school.

This was heavy on Ralph's heart when he and Ethel returned to Inhamaxafo for annual conference in 1940. They had been hesitant to leave Lundi long enough to go, but it proved to be good therapy for them to see their friends after a year of isolation. The Portuguese East Africa church was encouraged by Ralph's report of new converts and the successful ministry of their own evangelists. The African WMS was thrilled with Ethel's account of her work; and for the first time since they had organized, the African women voted to release the money they had been hoarding and to use it to spread the gospel.

When Ralph presented the need for a teacher at Lundi Central School, Miss Daisy Frederick, who was teaching in the Girls' School at Inhamaxafo, said she had already felt the call to Rhodesia and had just been waiting for the right time to go. It was obviously the right time, and she gladly agreed to return with Ralph and Ethel.

Traveling in the cab of a pickup truck for four days over miserable roads was not a restful experience, but Daisy learned that with the Jacobses, it was at least blessed with humor. Ralph's stories made the miles gallop, and animals on the road provided additional entertainment. Ralph could never resist seeing how fast an animal could run, and if it were an impala, he knew the right moment to hoot his horn so it would leap like a graceful dancer, then bound off through the bush. Even necessary "bush stops" brought a smile when Ralph called out, "Who wants to hunt gold?"

Living was easier for Ralph and Ethel after they returned from conference, because they brought back some of the household goods they had been doing without — a trunk of bedding, some pictures, the little pump organ Ethel had missed so much, her sewing machine, and one rocking chair. Ethel particularly enjoyed that chair, until a houseboy fell over it in the dark and broke a rocker. Then they put the chair away to wait for a new rocker to be hewn out of a tree. Ethel said it gave her opportunity to take joyfully the spoiling of her goods. However, she admitted that she had not felt very joyful when she discovered her broken chair.

Daisy took over Lundi School immediately and loved it

from the start. Class was held in the church, with the pupils sitting — or trying to sit — on the backless benches. Many of them had to be shown how. Supplies were a bare minimum. Most of the students had a slate and a pencil. The teacher had a chair, two small portable blackboards, a table, a cupboard, and some Rhodesian plan books (which Daisy understood only faintly). But she had much joy, knowing she was right where God wanted her to be.

The new missionary needed a residence. A growing school would have to have adequate classrooms and dormitories, and Ralph set to the task of providing those needs. His wisdom was demonstrated in his long-range plan for the station and in the skillful manner in which he built. His philosophy had been formed in South Africa and tested in Portuguese East Africa. Ralph understood the basic fact that missionaries are human. He said:

> Every missionary family needs privacy. Homes should be separated by enough distance so that troubles won't arise over such things as pets and children, etc.

Ralph's eye for beauty led him to choose the most lovely setting possible for each residence, and he built with simplicity of style, getting the job done with whatever funds were available, which was usually less than one would consider adequate.

Wide, airy verandas kept his houses as cool as possible in summer. His well-constructed fireplaces provided necessary warmth in the winter. Floors were made of cement to prevent termites, except when cement was unobtainable. Walls were cement block or burned brick, plastered over and painted yellow, because "yellow repels mosquitoes." Woodwork was always painted dark green. Behind each house he dug a large cistern for storing rain water, and he planted citrus trees on every station. These essentials, he said, were to protect the missionaries' health. Extras would only create additional barriers between the white man and the African.

Daisy loved her three-room cottage near the hippo pools in Lundi River. It was built on a slightly raised area of partially exposed granite rocks and was sheltered by shady trees. Occasionally, hippos roamed the paths around her house at night, but that did not trouble Daisy.

When Lundi School opened the following January, the African teacher took the little children, while Daisy taught the older ones and some young men who wished to be trained for the pastorate. These men were new converts, and none of them had ever been to school before. They could write a little, more or less legibly, and they could read the Bible stumblingly, but they felt God had called them to win souls. More than anything else, they wanted to learn how to be effective workers for God. Daisy was full of enthusiasm for such a class as that!

By August, Ralph had completed the school building and there was great excitement when the students saw long desks — with benches attached — and wide, ample blackboards. "This is *doropa!*" they said. ("This is the city!") But to those from America, Lundi was still a primitive place.

Huge window spaces looked out onto virgin forest, and one day the African teacher watched a python swallow a bushbuck. Hippos munched their way through the school garden at night. From time to time, Ralph shot one of them for trespassing, and it furnished meat for the missionaries and boarding students. Occasionally, a kudu met with the same fate. Crocodiles sometimes dragged dogs and cows to their death in the river, which was the school's water supply. But these events only livened the students' conversation around their fires at night when the lessons of the day were done.

* * * * * * * * *

The Jacobses had assumed when they went to Southern Rhodesia, that after a year or two, they would take their overdue furlough. Now they were ready. The last two hot seasons had been harder on them than any since they had been in Africa. In fact, they were so weary that little difficulties, normally faced without thought, were assuming momentous proportions. For their own sakes, as well as for the good of the work, they needed to rest. However, World War II had made it necessary to cancel all overseas furloughs for African missionaries. Ralph and Ethel could not go to America, but they could rest in South Africa if someone would take their places at Lundi.

The Reverend and Mrs. Laurence Arksey, who were furloughing in South Africa at the time, were asked to sacrifice six months of their furlough to work in Rhodesia so the Jacobses could have six months of rest. Arkseys were not only willing but challenged by the idea, and they came in time for Ralph and Ethel to leave just as the intense heat of summer was beginning.

It was turning cold in Johannesburg when the Jacobses arrived there. For several weeks they spent the days wrapped in blankets, with hot water bottles in their laps or at their feet. Then they moved to Pretoria where it was warmer. But the rushing city was noisy and crowded. The pavements were hard, and when they saw a bit of open, green country, they felt the urge to flee for home. However, the food was good, there was no need for daily quinine, and they found rest from pressing schedules. Their spirits and bodies were refreshed. By February, 1943, they were back at Lundi, where the grunting hippos, the song of the doves, and even the repeated knocks at the door were welcome sounds.

War not only curtailed overseas travel, it also brought gas rationing to Rhodesia and that severely limited use of the mission vehicle. For the first time in all their years in Africa, Ethel could not go with Ralph on his school inspections and church visits. Instead of the truck, he used a car or bicycle, and Ethel stayed home. She missed being out with the people, but she was not idle. From her little hut dispensary, which Ralph had built in their backyard, Ethel treated the sick. She was also teaching the women to read, sew, and memorize scripture.

Ethel's first contact with the primitive Shangaan women around Lundi had given her little reason to believe they could ever be brought out of the rough. But she knew from experience that the gospel has power to transform lives. As they became converted, changes began to occur, not only in their hearts, but in their appearance. Their faces showed joy. They took off the dirty strings around their necks and waists, which held charms from the witch doctor. Their bodies were washed clean and black. Instead of beer and dancing, they enjoyed coming to worship.

These women's homes were scattered miles from the mission, making individual contact impossible, so Ethel invited them to the mission two days a week for instruction. They responded to this enthusiastically. Each woman bought her own slate, pencil, and primer — and arrived the first day with a baby on her back and a small child or two by her side. Ethel's veranda was soon inadequate, and they moved to the church.

They had to be taught the correct way to sit on a bench, to be quiet instead of talking whenever they wanted to, and to stand when reciting their lessons. Their hands, stiff from working in the fields, had to learn how to hold a pencil and guide it on paper. But these women wanted to learn, and in spite of every obstacle — even crying babies — they learned. Their expressions of incredulous joy when they read a word correctly for the first time, and realized the page was speaking to them, was more than enough reward.

As soon as they finished their first reader, Ethel began to teach them from their Testaments. Thus a Bible class developed, and that had been her intention from the start. As they studied the book of John, the Holy Spirit opened His Word to them. One day, after studying about the woman of Samaria, Ethel asked if they would be willing to witness to their friends if God called their husbands into evangelistic work. Some of them answered yes; and not long afterward, when God called three of their husbands to be evangelists, those women were ready and willing to go. To Ralph and Ethel, sending out those first three pastors was a significant milestone. It was also convincing proof of answered prayer to their plea for laborers in the harvest.

Those three young men were products of Daisy Frederick's class. The first one was sent many miles from Lundi to a struggling group of believers who had never had a resident pastor. They received him joyfully enough, and provided him with a few crude articles of housekeeping — a water pot, a clay cooking pot, and wooden spoons. But they knew nothing about supporting him. His utter dependence upon God for daily food was a severe test. When he returned to Lundi to move his wife to their new home, he was discouraged and asked the missionaries for financial help. The missionaries felt deeply for him; but they remained steadfast in the belief that if the church were to grow strong, it would have to be self-supporting, and the evangelists would have to learn to trust God for their needs. They talked and prayed with this young man and assured him of their continuing prayers, and he left, sadly. But the next Sunday when he preached to his congregation, his face was radiant and peaceful. He told the people that he had been ready to give up because he did not see how he could live. Then God had said:

> Is it not you who were saved from your sin and given eternal life? Then you cannot fail to go and carry this salvation to others.

Within a few months, many people were converted, including an aged witch doctor. More and more outstations opened around that church, and a helper was needed to care for them.

The second student also struggled to find the courage to trust for his support. He had two elderly relatives who were dependent upon him, besides his wife and two tiny children. The support pledged by the church was less than two dollars a month, plus house and gardens. The young man went to the Lord in prayer, and step by step, the way opened before him. His older, invalid brother was saved, and the church began to take on the pastor's support.

The third man went without hesitation to his church. He said,

> I don't like to go with so little support, but I am going because my heart compels me.

And God blessed his ministry.

* * * * * * * * * *

Ralph and Ethel never ceased to marvel during those first five years as they saw the transforming power of God changing people's lives. The men who had worked for Ralph in the beginning had been, in his words, "a wild, red-eyed, snuff-chewing, half-naked lot of people, drawn to the mission largely because of a desire to earn tax money, and incidentally, to see what new thing was going on in their country." Within a few, short years, they were sober, saved men, living the Christian life with their families, before their heathen neighbors. Old Tambo was one of many.

Tambo lived near Maranda School and dressed in a goatskin which hung from his loins. At special times, he wore an old shirt and a broad-brimmed, high-crowned hat he had woven from reeds. His son, Simon, who had been one of the first converts at Lundi, invited him to church. But Tambo would not go. He was, however, friendly toward the African pastor and the missionaries when they came to visit.

Ralph usually camped near Tambo's village when he inspected Maranda School. In the evening, Tambo and his wife liked to come over and *bula* (exchange the latest news) with the white man. Before they left, Ralph and Ethel would sing a hymn, read the Word, and have prayer. Later, Tambo began to attend church, and he finally accepted the Saviour. The dramatic changes in his appearance and behavior were proof to his heathen neighbors of his new life.

One day Tambo's faith was severely tested when a large puff adder bit him on the foot while he was working alone in the field. He shook off the snake and tried to go to the evangelist's house. But by the time people found him, he was delirious and near death. It was fifty miles to Lundi. The people did not know what to do, except to send a runner to the trading store with the hope of finding snake-bite medicine. Then the evangelist knelt and prayed for God to save Tambo's life. Before the messenger returned, Tambo was conscious and rational. The crisis was passed. The usually slow-healing wound closed within a week, and God received praise.

Another convert won out of paganism was Haklane Chauke, whom Ralph hired as a kitchen boy to trek with him when he supervised building on the outstations. Haklane proved to be a poor cook, so he was "promoted" to masonry and building. That he enjoyed and did well. Before long, Haklane was converted. While he built, the urge to preach grew within him until he was finally released to preach full time.

Jona Chibaya, who was one of Ralph's first laborers, asked hesitantly one day whether he might become a Christian. The answer he received was encouraging, so he went home to think about it. He said later that "a still small voice" began to instruct him and lead him into the light of salvation. Then he entered Lundi School and as he studied the Word, the "still small voice" told him to go tell his people. He began by sharing in nearby villages. A witch doctor was converted. Before long, he had a regular preaching assignment. For the remainder of his life Jona continued to be a faithful and powerful evangelist.

Women who were converted became effective witnesses to their pagan husbands. Boys and girls who found the Lord served as Sunday school teachers. And so, lives were changed and the good news was spread. Within the first five years, there were 650 church members.

It may be interesting to note here Ralph's personal philosophy regarding church growth.

> ... Man has very little to do in the "saving" process, apart from giving knowledge of a Saviour. ... The church must shine, but that is all it can do to make a true increase and save souls. ...
>
> If I were to give a recipe for church growth, I would say this: "Much prayer for guidance of the Holy Spirit. Then throw all your resources into getting the work done to prepare for an increase, using, of course, the best judgment in planning for this increase." God only knows where the people are whose hearts are hungry and thirsty, and the guidance to reach them with the light must come from Him. I, myself, never worried about the fruit and the increase. I was more concerned as to how I planned and worked in harmony with the Holy Spirit. ...
>
> I think it pays well in the end in mission work to put a great share of effort in helping our indigenous workers to grow spiritually. ...

The period of great additions and increases in the church finally gave place to a period of Christian growth, of teaching, leading, and perfecting. Of course, there were disappointments. Some converts, and even some pastors and teachers, returned to lives of sin. Satan does not give up his territory easily, and Ralph and Ethel were always aware that they were working in Satan's territory. But Ralph did not allow such disappointments to dim his faith nor his confidence in God. He wore no rose-tinted glasses to hide and excuse the failures of his fellowmen. Neither did he criticize and condemn. Where others loved, forgave, and left it at that, Ralph loved, forgave, and tried to train and lift men to the level he knew was possible through the grace of God.

Ralph's personal standard of Christian living was high and strict, and he adhered closely to it. But he never expected from others more than he demanded of himself.

As a missionary, he said it was his responsibility to set an example of godliness.

> Africans will never wonder why we don't accomplish certain things, but if we don't show patience and love, then all our work is straw and stubble. My prayer is for an abundance of the three missionary requisites — patience, love, and courage.

Ralph's life was characterized by those three graces. Furthermore, Ralph had learned to think "black."

> ... There is a tendency among us whites to be too hasty in criticizing the religious experiences of our black brothers because they don't act just like we think they should act, nor repent just like white folks repent; or perhaps they don't react to truth just like some other races react. Our experience has been that the raw heathen doesn't break with the past because of high emotional pressures of revivals. As a rule, he doesn't suddenly turn about-face and make far-reaching decisions.... Perhaps it is because his fathers for ages have been traveling along this same path in the same direction; or perhaps, just because his head doesn't think as we think he ought to think.... The African, receiving new ways and light, acts much like a grazing cow. He puts truth away and ruminates it later at his leisure. Instead of rushing down the church aisle, throwing himself across a mourners' bench, and struggling through to a knowledge of sins forgiven, he is much more apt to quietly rise in meeting and say, "I choose the Lord."... The "going forward" is usually preceded by far-reaching decisions made all by himself.... To him, the altar is more the place of a public confession of something already done in his heart. Afterwards, the altar is freely used as a place of confession if he has side-stepped, or a place of renewing his covenant with God; and especially, it is a place for receiving help in times of trouble and trial.

The trials of these African Christians are just as fiery to them as the trials of the white Christian, although many times, along entirely different lines. . . . For instance, fear is often the cause of many of the black man's actions. Fear of evil spirits, fear of the unknown, fear of incurring the displeasure of the ancestral spirits. Any departure from the normal life, such as sudden sickness, is an indication that displeasure has been incurred, for which the only known remedy is to invoke the power of the witch doctor. . . .

Yes, there are real Christians in our African church. Of course, there are some backsliders among them — and compromisers and time-servers and lukewarm professors. If there were not these, we would doubt the presence in Africa of a personal devil. However, we must not get our eyes on the one who failed and forget the man who is plodding on daily in the steps of Jesus. Yes, African Christians live good and die victoriously. . . . There is already a cemetery at this new Lundi Mission and the Christians have died well. Let us pray more for our African Christians that their number may increase, and that they, together with their missionaries, may be a witness to the world that God is no respecter of persons.

Ethel's Christian character was also worthy of imitation. Through her ability to counsel, comfort, and teach with love, many were strengthened in the faith. She adhered faithfully to her personal convictions regarding dress, yet she was wise enough not to impose her convictions on the African women.

One day at Lundi, a young African woman came to church wearing silk stockings. After service Ethel told her that she should not try to imitate the white people by wearing such things. Stockings, she said, were expensive, hot, and got holes easily. Besides, it was a pity to cover such beautiful black skin. The woman took Ethel's advice, and it was years before the inevitable encroachment of civilization brought wearing of hose into common practice among the educated African women.

When Ralph began to hold circuit business meetings, he was pleased to see how quickly and naturally the people responded to the instructions from the *Discipline* — one person speaking at a time without interruption, listening to the chairman, proposing matters to the body, seconding, and voting. It was all so new. Yet with little problem, stewards and Sunday school superintendents were elected, and men were recommended to the quarterly conference for preachers' licenses.

As Rhodesian converts took their places in the church, the Portuguese East Africa evangelists gradually returned home, having accomplished their purpose.

* * * * * * * * * *

Lundi Central School flourished under Miss Daisy Frederick's leadership. Ruth Smith joined the staff in 1944. Outstation schools were gradually added in the reserve and churches continued to spring up. As the mission grew, so did Ralph's responsibilities. He was the builder and hunter. He was the district superintendent of the churches, making quarterly visits to each one. He was the school inspector, hiring teachers for all the kraal schools and planning the course of instruction. He inspected each classroom four times a year to see that plans were being carried out. He inspected the school gardens and the pupils' handwork and sent regular reports to the government.

All of this called for many miles of travel, and money was never plentiful. There were days when Ralph's faith kept the car running. His approach to God was direct and simple. Before starting on a trip he was once heard to pray:

> Dear Father, you know that the tires on this truck are not very good. We have not had the money to replace them. If you will keep them strong, I'll try my best to

keep from hitting any rough stones or stumps in the road. Thank you.

And God rewarded his faith.

Ralph's disciplined life-style, his ability to organize, and his habit of punctuality made it possible for him to keep his rigorous schedule. His punctuality was one habit everyone learned to recognize and respect. To Ralph, "on time" meant being half an hour early. If he said he would leave at 5:30, he would start the car by 5:00, and leave by 5:15. More than one African who was planning to go with him arrived just in time to see the car disappear down the road.

Other missionaries said that Africans could not help being late because they had only the sun to guide them. Ralph believed Africans could learn to be punctual, but he did not expect them to do what he did not. For that reason, Ralph told time by the sun rather than by a watch, and he did it with great accuracy.

* * * * * * * * * *

The basic groundwork of opening Matibi No. 1 Reserve was just about complete by 1945, and the Lundi area was becoming almost too civilized for Ralph to feel comfortable. He told Ethel one day that he had met a car on the road, so it must be about time for them to move on.

More and more, Ralph's attention was drawn to Matibi No. 2 Reserve where the government had granted one hundred acres for a new mission station. This new site, Chikombedzi (which was first known as Nuanetsi), was located in flat, dry bushland near the Portuguese East Africa border, ninety miles southeast of Lundi and that much further from civilization. But it was also that much nearer to Chief Sengwe's village. Ralph was ready to go as soon as another missionary couple could be sent to Lundi.

While he waited, Ralph sent Philip Mberane, a Portuguese East Africa evangelist, on ahead to open a church at Chikombedzi. A small kraal school was also begun. Philip's church class of inquirers consisted chiefly of the boys and girls from the school. There seemed to be no better foundation for a church than school children who took home to their pagan families the things they learned each day.

By the time the Reverend and Mrs. Eldon Sayre arrived in 1946, restrictions had been lifted on overseas travel, and the Jacobses were making plans for a furlough in America. It would soon be fourteen years since they had been home. But before they left, Ralph wanted to drill the well at Chikombedzi so that when they returned, all would be ready for him to build.

Within six weeks of Sayres' arrival, Ralph and Ethel were on their way to Chikombedzi. In the pickup with them were their African helpers, their dog and two cats, and supplies to last for several months. They had checked their list carefully before leaving. They knew they could not return easily for forgotten items.

Chikombedzi was not the sort of place one might expect to find a couple who were approaching their sixties. The trip, itself, was an unforgettable experience. The last fifty miles was a dirt track which crossed numerous bridgeless creek beds, and it changed with the weather. No beautiful river flowed year around near Chikombedzi Mission. No lush growth, no lofty koppies against blue sky. No hippos, either. But there were elephants, lions, and all the other wild game, both large and small, to add a touch of danger. Yet Ralph was eager. For Ethel, the move meant sacrifice. She was suffering now from rheumatoid arthritis, and being shaken over those roads in a pickup truck was far from comforting to her swollen, painful joints. Neither was camping any longer a pleasure. But she went with Ralph, gladly.

The fact that lions were in the area did not prevent them from living in a tent while Ralph built two temporary huts, one for sleeping, one for eating. The weather was turning cooler, but conditions were generally better than when they had camped at Lundi seven years earlier.

Progress on the well went slowly. Rock was just under the surface. And it was hard and thick. With prayer and patience, sweat and toil, they went down, bit by bit, dynamite blast by dynamite blast. Dig, blast, then dig some more.

Ethel was more aware of their isolation at Chikombedzi than she had been anywhere else. Perhaps it was because she could no longer accompany Ralph on all of his trips.

> July 3, 1946
>
> Friday was a big day for me. I had been here alone for a day and a half — alone as far as any other white person being in the country for miles around — as Mr. Jacobs had gone to Lundi for more supplies. About one o'clock he drove in with post, which contained letters from our mothers and from all the ladies at the Lundi station, as well as other local letters, two *Free Methodists,* the June *Missionary Tidings,* five *YPMS News,* our radio, fresh vegetables, eggs, and butter. Do you wonder it was an exciting afternoon? It seemed we had been cut off from the rest of the world for weeks . . . soon had our aerial up, and about the first news we heard was that Britons were going on a bread ration. Those brave people! . . . After reading our papers, it seemed as if we had had a visit around the world. . . .

Ralph and Ethel had folded their tent and were living in their pole-and-mud houses when Missionary Secretary Byron S. Lamson stopped in Southern Rhodesia a few months later on his round-the-world tour of Free Methodist Missions. Ralph drove out the long distance to meet him at Beit Bridge and found him anticipating his visit to Free Methodism's newest mission station. Chikombedzi was Dr. Lamson's first taste of African bush life, and it was just as he had imagined — two mud-floored, thatched-roofed huts, and venison roast for dinner.

On tour of the mission, Dr. Lamson was impressed by all that had been accomplished in so short a time. The garage-storeroom was completed, and in back of that was a lean-to which served as a schoolroom for thirty pupils. He visited Evangelist Philip Mberane's village and the well-drilling site. There the workmen told Ralph that while he was away to get Dr. Lamson, water had come into the well. The full significance of that news dawned on Dr. Lamson the following morning when Ralph prayed at family worship.

Ralph prayed around the world and back again. He prayed for the heathen in their darkness. He prayed for his fellow missionaries, the pastors, evangelists, the teachers. Then he prayed, "Lord, remember the men with the dynamite, working on the well. Help us to find wat —" Ralph paused, remembering that they had already found water. Dr. Lamson peeked and saw great tears rolling down Ralph's sunburned cheeks, and he heard him falter, choke a little, and then pray on, "We do thank Thee for the water. We do thank Thee. Give us good water, sweet water, and may the stream be plentiful. We thank Thee, O Lord, for water."

Chikombedzi Mission was officially opened that day, and five hundred Africans attended the service, most of them heathen who understood little of the message. But the Spirit of God was present, and the Word would eventually bear much fruit.

* * * * * * * * * *

Back at Lundi, Eldon and Florence Sayre found themselves with a bigger job than they had expected. They had all of Ralph's previous duties, which included building their own house, and all the while they were learning the language and adjusting to a new culture, a new climate, and not least of all, to their first baby, Margaret Ann, born just two months after they arrived in Africa. But they survived and thrived.

At the end of that year, Ralph and Ethel left on furlough as scheduled, and a week or two later, Miss Daisy Frederick passed away. Her death was not expected. It brought a sense of shock and deep sadness. Daisy had been a beautiful character, happy, energetic, and devoted. She was greatly loved both by the Africans and her missionary family. She died in the hospital in Fort Victoria, but her African friends requested that her body be brought back to Lundi and buried among them in the mission's Christian cemetery. Their request was granted.

News of Daisy's death reached Ralph and Ethel while they were still in Durban arranging passage. A few days later, a second message brought them word that Ethel's mother had passed away. They had been eager to leave because they knew Mrs. Lightner was ill. Now she was gone. Their voyage was a sad one, but God comforted their hearts and refreshed their spirits during their short, six-month furlough in America.

The weight of responsibility on Eldon's shoulders during Ralph's absence was made heavier by a severe famine. All around them the people were suffering from hunger. Even the animals were dying as rivers dried up and the grazing land was finished. Hundreds of young men left their villages and went to the cities to work so they could send home money for food. Church offerings became almost nonexistent as the people had less and less to eat. The evangelists were destitute.

In response to this desperate situation, the Mission Board sent famine relief funds and authorized Eldon to purchase corn for the evangelists and others in need. It came "like a burst of light in the night," Eldon wrote. And though it meant miles and miles of extra traveling, he was glad to be able to sustain their lives.

* * * * * * * * *

Medical work at Lundi officially began in 1947 with the arrival of a missionary nurse, Nina Detwiler. Ethel's mud hut "clinic" was gratefully turned over to her, complete with its furnishings — a table, a chair, and a cupboard — all made from packing crates. The drug supply was basically a bottle of aspirin, sulfathiazole tablets (then permissible), eye ointment, anti-malarial medication, and a set of dental forceps which Ralph had used when teeth needed to be extracted. How much comfort and healing those simple medicines had brought through the years! But now, with a qualified nurse, the mission would receive government financial assistance, and the Mission Board would appropriate funds so that, in time, an adequate clinic would be built and equipped.

At first, Nina saw only five or six patients a day, which was probably fortunate. She was studying the language and teaching a first aid course at Lundi School. But then a difficult case came which tested her skill and courage and firmly established her reputation in the community.

The patient was a woman in labor, unable to deliver. Nina quickly recognized that it would not be a normal delivery and sent a messenger to call an ambulance from town, seventy miles away. Forty-eight hours later, the ambulance arrived, too late. Triplets had been born. Two were living, but the mother had stopped breathing. Nina could no longer detect a pulse. The African ambulance driver entered the hut and declared that the patient was dead. But Nina continued to work over her; and Ruth Smith, who had been assisting, continued to pray. Suddenly the patient opened her eyes and began to talk. She refused to go to the hospital in the ambulance, and the astonished driver went outside and announced to the people, "She lives!" News of this miracle spread, and people came from near and far to see the mother and her babies. From that time on, the number of patients increased rapidly.

For years, Nina's helper was an African woman who had only one or two years of schooling. Later, three graduates from Lundi Central School were sent away for nurses' training at another mission hospital, and they returned to work at Lundi Clinic.

* * * * * * * * *

Ralph and Ethel's final term of service began at Chikombedzi. Opposition was encountered from the start, but they saw that as a sign of victory ahead, because they said,

> ... When Satan's domain is invaded, he always puts up a good fight. Wife and I have now been here over six weeks.... We have had great difficulty in getting local transportation for bringing building materials from the river, three miles away. In vain I searched before I came down here for an old truck chassis that could be converted into a wagon.... I contacted Mr. Palfry on the P.E.A. border, and he gave me an old 3-ton Ford chassis if I would take it from there myself.... Delays in getting donkeys, harness, etc., held up this matter until three days ago when I finally succeeded in sending the donkeys to bring the chassis over fifty-five miles of bad road. If they escape the lions and are not molested by elephants, they should return this week....

Some days Ethel found it difficult to be patient until Ralph could finish their house. The garage, which served as a temporary home, was crowded with building supplies as well as themselves. Dust blew in freely through the open rafters. Hordes of flies and mosquitoes flew in. Hot season came on, bringing the temperature to a fairly constant 100°. It also brought rain. But the rain brought prospects of a good harvest, and after so much famine, that made the heat more bearable.

Following one particularly heavy rain, the first nurse for Chikombedzi, Miss Virginia Strait, arrived at Lundi. It was nine days before the ground was dry enough for the Jacobses to go out for her. Driving back to Chikombedzi was Virginia's unforgettable initiation to bush roads.

The trip was only about one hundred miles, but it took

us nearly twelve hours. The roads were either washed in or washed out, so they were rebuilt during the course of the trip. I now understand the words of David Livingstone when he said: "Anywhere, just so it is forward." However, nothing daunts the spirits of Mr. Jacobs, his motto being: "I will find a way or make one." The walking was not crowded, so Mrs. Jacobs and I lightened the load by walking across the strategic points. . . .

With good humor, Ralph and Ethel squeezed Virginia into the garage to live with them. And for a temporary clinic, Ralph built a pole-and-mud hut like the one he had built at Lundi for Ethel. Virginia felt right at home under the thatched roof, and she dispensed her medicines with a smile and generous doses of love. Her first patients were those who had not been cured by the witch doctor or who were sure they would die anyway. It takes time for primitive people to trust the white man's medicine.

* * * * * * * * * *

In those early days, the lion population around Chikombedzi made it necessary for Ralph to protect his cattle at night. To do this, he constructed a circular cattle kraal behind the garage, made of tall poles, leaning outward. Outside of this, he built a high, thick, thorn fence with wire cable nooses inserted every twenty feet. Outside of that was a second thorn fence with nooses in strategic places. In the passageway between, was a small pen for a donkey which served as lion bait. Over the years Ralph never lost a cow, nor even a frightened donkey, but he snared five hungry lions.

One night when a trapped lion began to roar, Virginia, who had a phobia for Ethel's house cats, ran fearlessly out of doors to watch the excitement. Ralph managed to get her into the truck and drive her near the kraal where she watched in safety while the lion lunged and roared and the donkey brayed — before Ralph shot the lion and peace was restored.

The next morning, when the African schoolteacher did not appear at school, Ralph found him still hiding in fright on the garage roof. He would not be coaxed down until Ralph convinced him that the lion really was dead.

Another morning when Ralph went out to kill a snared lion, he lifted the gun to shoot, then lowered it and sheepishly called back to the house, "Ethel, bring my glasses!" Ethel found his glasses, put them on his nose, and Ralph shot the lion. Ever after, he enjoyed telling that story on himself. In fact, he had several favorite stories that were always good for a chuckle.

One was of the night years before at Inhamaxafo, Portuguese East Africa, when he saw the eyes of an animal gleaming in the path ahead of him. Thinking it was a spring hare that would taste good for dinner, he shot, then ran to claim his *nyama* (meat). On the path lay Ethel's dead pussy cat instead. At that point in the story, Ethel always interrupted Ralph to say, "Yes, it was my poor, poor pussy cat."

Hunting was not usually humorous. More often, it was just hard work. Although it served as a welcome diversion from his other mission duties, Ralph never hunted for sport alone. He hunted to provide food for his family, and when necessary, to destroy predators. Sometimes, while hunting elephant and buffalo, he was brought close to death.

The cape buffalo is considered to be the most dangerous of all African animals to hunt because of its tendency to turn on the hunter, and a fatal frontal shot is almost impossible due to the thick, wide horn that covers its head. Sam, an African who frequently hunted with Ralph, remembers well the time a lone buffalo bull they were following turned on them and charged. The other two trackers ran in panic and climbed the nearest tree, while Sam stayed close to Ralph and the gun. Ralph bravely stood his ground, firing repeatedly at the charging bull, until it finally dropped dead only a few yards from his feet.

* * * * * * * * * *

There were no regrets when the house was finally finished and they moved out of the dusty garage. The new, two-bedroom, burned-brick residence had been built with the incredibly small amount of $1,500. It was designed for comfort in hot weather, with wide, screened-in verandas on both sides. In the kitchen was a small, black, wood cooking stove, and Ethel's *first* refrigerator, one that ran on kerosene. The bathroom was a room and a path: a room inside for bathing with Ralph's custom-made bucket shower, and a path leading to the privy behind the house. There was no running water, but a two-wheeled cart with two 55-gallon drums of water attached was parked handily outside the kitchen door. When this ran dry, it was pushed to the well a quarter of a mile away, pumped full by hand, then towed back to the house with the car. A small 1,500-watt generator, purchased with gift money from a friend, made possible one bare light bulb in each room. When necessary, these could be used for a few hours in the evening instead of the kerosene lamps. Situated as it was, on a slight rise in otherwise flat terrain, this house in the wilderness seemed to symbolize for them the city that is set on a hill and cannot be hid.

But that was not the end of building for Ralph. A single ladies' residence was needed, and beyond Virginia's tiny hut-clinic, Ralph envisioned a fine hospital, serving both reserves.

In June, 1949, when Ralph had completed the first three small clinic rooms, he staged such an impressive opening celebration that after twenty-three years, Makanani, an African lady who attended, gave Dr. Paul Embree this vivid version of the grand occasion. She said:

> Mufundisi Jacobi killed four animals. He bought two hundred pounds of cornmeal and some salt, and he called all the people to come for a feast. They came, filling the whole yard. Mufundisi cut the meat and ordered it to be cooked, and he gave out the salt to be

used. When they had eaten, he gathered the people together behind the new clinic and told them about the gospel.

To illustrate his message, he used some of them to act out a simple play. He tied a black cloth around Sam and told him to lie down and pretend to be ill. Dumela was to be the witch doctor and throw the bones. Sam's wife was to be a demon, standing behind the witch doctor. Then a white cloth was tied around Makanani to represent God in heaven, and she stood behind the man who pretended to be the doctor. The doctor put a thermometer into Sam's mouth and pretended to give him an injection. Sam got well. The play ended.

Then Mufundisi asked, "Who did the better job, the one who threw the bones, or the man who gave medicine?"

The people answered, "The doctor."

Then Mufundisi asked, "Who stood behind the doctor?"

The people responded, "God."

"What does God do?" Mufundisi asked. And he answered, "He gives power."

"Did the demon help?"

"No," the people replied.

Then Mufundisi asked the people whom they would follow, and he urged them to leave their spirits and follow God. After that, the clinic door was opened and the people were invited to come for medicine.

It was years before the truth of Ralph's message penetrated Makanani's understanding, but she finally chose the Lord with her whole heart. To symbolize her new life, she chose a new name, Mamani Ella. Today, Mamani Ella is a strong and beautiful witness to the power of Jesus.

In January, 1950, the first doctor, Dr. Naomi Pettengill, arrived at Chikombedzi with boundless energy and ingenuity. Together with Virginia, she set to the task of organizing a functioning hospital in that exceedingly primitive setting, a task which took years to complete and was shared by the doctors who followed after her.

There was no running water. The equipment was inadequate and there were only primitive Africans to assist with the work. Patients were beginning to come from many miles around, on bicycle, on foot, and by ox cart.

Ralph added two simple rooms onto the clinic to make space for twelve, cot-size beds. Each patient brought his blanket, food, cooking pot, and a relative to cook for him during the length of his stay. An outpatient village, consisting of a few pole-and-grass huts, provided scanty shelter for relatives and outpatients.

Sometimes the missionaries were requested to bring seriously ill patients to the hospital in the mission vehicle. But more often, they remained in distant villages without treatment. Mobile clinics would help provide medical care for them, but considering the small staff, the distances, and the condition of the roads, that would be an ambitious undertaking. Nevertheless, plans were made, and the first mobile clinic proved to be as successful and satisfying as it was exhausting.

... Daniel is our three-quarter ton Chevrolet pickup which the Washington YPMS gave us last year. We call it Daniel because we find no fault in it, and because it isn't afraid of lions. Ever since Daniel arrived, we've waited for the day when we could start our mobile clinic work.

Mpapa is the big chief over this area. He has always been friendly to our work ... Mpapa is the village where God undertook so miraculously and saved Muhlava's life about a year ago, and now all the people acknowledge His work. Nearly every day we have patients who walk the twenty-five miles from that village, so we thought that would be a good, well-populated, easily accessible place to start the mobile work.

We sent word a week ahead and on September 27, we started out on our first mobile clinic. About eighteen miles up the road, a man came out and stopped us; he wanted medicine for colds, itch, and syphilis, for his crowd of twenty or thirty women and children gathered there. We didn't know how our medical supplies would hold out, so we told them to wait until we returned.

At Mpapa's village a crowd of 258 were gathered by the time we parked Daniel under a tree and set up our folding table. Evangelist Samson was mightily helped of the Lord as he gave a message and had prayer. They were there — the chief, a sub-chief, Muhlava, half-clothed women, tiny babies, small children, herd boys, giggling girls, skinny dogs, sharing the tiny bit of 90-degree shade with us, and in the periphery of the crowd, the cattle and goats that totally disregarded our procedures.

The acutely ill could be spotted by their woebegone expressions much more accurately than by stethoscope or thermometer, but most of the cases were colds, scabies, diarrhea, and sore eyes. We gave 201 treatments — one a minute! Chief Mpapa's gratitude was real when he came to tell us good-bye, and we promised to return in two weeks if rain didn't close the roads.

On the return trip we stopped to eat our lunch, and in a short time, fifty or sixty had gathered around the car. Again we availed ourselves of the chance to give the gospel as Samson spoke and prayed before we gave 53 treatments.

A man hailed us and asked us to see a very sick woman in his village nearby. She was an obese, white-haired old grandmother with malaria. ... This was probably the first prayer she had ever heard to a living God, and possibly she was too deaf and too ill to hear!

As Paul said about his work at Ephesus, "For a wide door for effective work has opened to me" (I Corinthians 16:9, RSV), so this is an open door for the message of salvation. Sickness and filth are all about us, and the people do have confidence in our medicine. If only they will accept the Great Physician as healer of their sin-sick hearts!

Mamani Tema, an African Christian from Portuguese East Africa, responded to Ralph's call for workers at Chikombedzi. She came on foot, a twenty-one day journey, from her home near Inhamaxafo. Tema, who had practical nurses' training, considered no task too menial for her to do. She gave medicine, washed clothes, and cleaned latrines. After her day's work was over, she walked miles to visit and pray with people in surrounding villages. When Ethel opened the Sunday school, Tema served as the first Sunday school superintendent at Chikombedzi. For more than twenty years, she worked faithfully, going home to visit only a few times. Finally, in the late 1960s, Tema felt her work in Rhodesia was finished, and as a gray-haired old lady, she returned home to Portuguese East Africa.

* * * * * * * * *

Even when Ralph first went to Chikombedzi, the great area of the Limpopo Valley was calling him. The government had granted the third and final mission site on the Nuanetsi River, fifty miles south of Chikombedzi, and Ralph had named it *Dumisa,* meaning "Praise." That station would complete the mission's coverage of Chief Sengwe's land, and Ralph was eager to see it established. However, the government required that a missionary be in residence, and that called for the appointment of the third missionary couple.

In 1948, the Reverend and Mrs. Tillman Houser and their two young sons had come to Rhodesia to be that third couple. By 1950, they had moved into the first two rooms of their Dumisa home. At last, there was a mission station near Chief Sengwe's village. Ralph's promise to the chief was fulfilled.

     * * * * * * * * *

But Ralph had one great disappointment. He had been unable to establish a Bible school in Rhodesia like the one at Inhamaxafo. There, a large area of land had been set aside where students could live with their families, plant their own gardens, have their own animals and be self-supporting. From the beginning, Ralph had looked for such a place in Rhodesia; but each time he thought he had found the right one, it was either not for sale or else the price was too high. This was hard for Ralph to understand. He knew a Bible school was an essential part of the mission program.

Eldon Sayre had been sent to Rhodesia to open the Bible school, but the continual shortage of staff and funds and the failure to find a suitable location had prevented it. In lieu of a regular school, Ralph had done what he could. Each year, when the men were not busy in their fields, Ralph had called his evangelists to the mission station for three to four weeks. During this time, he taught them reading, writing, arithmetic, Bible, how to be a pastor, and in general encouraged and counseled them. This was profitable and produced lasting results even though it was a substitute measure.

Ethel had been wanting to organize a Rhodesian branch of WMS so that the women would have something to do that was all their own. Traditionally, African women are considered to be of little importance, except to work for their husbands. As Christians, they needed to know that they had personal value in the kingdom of God.

With that in mind, Ethel, with the help of Gwen Houser, called the women together during the Annual Conference at Lundi, in 1952. They told them about the activities of the WMS in America and in other parts of Africa. And they suggested that the Rhodesian women could do evangelistic village visitation, a task for which they seemed naturally skilled. A president, secretary, and treasurer could be elected, as well as leaders for visitation. Once a month they could have a public meeting and give their reports. Dues were not to be required, but they could give what they felt they should to help spread the gospel.

Of course, the English name, Woman's Missionary Society, meant nothing to the Shangaans, so they chose the name *Vahlanganyeti,* which means, "Those who keep the fire burning." That had great significance to them because the fire is the center of African village life; and it is the woman's responsibility to keep the fire burning, not just while the food is cooking, but at other times, for warmth and light. Just so, in the church, the light of the gospel must be kept burning brightly for those who sit in darkness. The Rhodesian women saw that as part of their responsibility.

Eighteen charter members made up the Lundi Vahlanganyeti. Their secretary had never heard of taking minutes, but with Gwen's help, she learned. The treasurer did not know how to count money, but she was instructed to take it, after it had been counted by another, and give it into the safe keeping of the missionary. For the first few years, one of the missionary ladies acted as president.

As the women took to their task with zeal and diligence, God began to bless them. When roll was called at their first monthly meeting, every woman came forward with her offering of a *tickey* (three cents)! Not one gave only a penny. Ethel was amazed. That was a relatively large amount, and if given regularly, would equal the amount of their church dues.

Other Vahlanganyeti groups were organized throughout the two reserves, and at the end of the first year they reported more than $50 raised. To earn their money, some women had planted gardens and had given the proceeds. Others had sold grain or made baskets and pots. Best of all, six women had been won to the Lord. That year, three superintendents were elected to go over the district and organize new societies. The women's work was going and growing.

* * * * * * * * * *

All of his life, Ralph was a student. He had made it a practice to study carefully the land in which he lived and to draw maps of uncharted places. With his little telescope he studied the heavens. He was a careful observer of the animals and birds in the bush around him. He knew the plants and trees by name. From the Africans he gathered much valuable information about their culture and folklore. As a result, Ralph's judgment and advice were respected by all who knew him.

When the government survey team went through the Chikombedzi area to survey for a proposed railroad line from inland Rhodesia to Lourenço Marques, they stopped and asked Ralph his opinion of the best route through that part of the country. Later, the railway was built as he had suggested.

The Missionary Board deferred to Ralph's advice in matters of personnel, buildings, cars, and appropriations. They knew that when he asked for a certain thing, it was essential. And he usually received what he requested. In 1950 his name was submitted for a possible appointment as Secretary for Africa. When Ralph was informed of this, he responded as follows:

> I thank you for desiring to suggest my name for this position. I appreciate your confidence. However, I am unable to accept such an assignment. I am a missionary, and the appointment would cut me off from close contact with my chosen people. I am not yet prepared to relinquish my position in the front-line trenches for one of general superintendency. There are other reasons for not receiving such an appointment, but to me, the above is sufficient for refusing. . . .

* * * * * * * * * *

Around 1953, the government began to move people

from more densely populated urban areas into the sparsely populated Matibi No. 2 Reserve. Until then, scarcity of water had caused the primitive Shangaans to settle near the rivers, leaving large areas unoccupied. In preparation for these new settlers, the government drilled "bore holes" every two miles throughout the reserve. Then several hundred families were brought in by truck loads and deposited, with their belongings, onto virgin land, where they were to build new villages and plow new fields.

Those who resettled in the Dumisa area were of the Ndebele tribe and belonged chiefly to the Brethren in Christ Church and the Salvation Army. By mutual consent, their missionaries gave them over into the care of the Free Methodist Mission.

The people who were moved into the Chikombedzi area were mostly Vakaranga from the Wesleyan Methodist and Dutch Reform churches. Some of them joined the Free Methodist Church. Others formed new churches of their own, but all of them used Free Methodist schools and hospitals.

These changes were disruptive. The settlers felt like strangers in a strange land. Their grandfathers had been bitter enemies of the Shangaans, and now they found themselves neighbors to the Shangaan, drawing water from the same wells, plowing adjacent fields, and attending the same schools and churches. It took time for them to adjust to their new homeland — and time for the Shangaans to accept their new neighbors.

It was a time of adjustment for the missionaries as well. The Mandebele and Vakaranga people were more sophisticated than the primitive Shangaan. Their clothing was European. They were accustomed to sending their children to school and to using medical services. As a result, school enrollments, church attendance, and hospital and clinic patients increased. No longer was there only one African language group to serve. There were now three. Gradually worship services became multilingual.

Vakaranga and Mandebele teachers were incorporated into the school system. New missionaries coming to the field chose to learn the language they would need most in their particular line of work. A few missionaries with linguistic talent learned all three languages. By 1960, the population served by the Free Methodist Church, which had been estimated originally to be ten thousand, was approximately one hundred thousand.

* * * * * * * * * *

Time to retire crept up on Ralph and Ethel all too quickly. By the way Ralph was working, he did not appear to be ready for retirement; and indeed, his heart was not. From letters to his mother, it was clear he had not slowed his pace.

April 11, 1952

Tomorrow is our wedding anniversary, 41 years ago!... It looks rainy this evening. We are at a District Meeting, camping under a big fig tree and sleeping in the car....

October 21, 1954

We have just finished a large Lundi Central School building — four large classrooms and an office. The old, original, grass-covered buildings have been torn down. This new building will meet the needs of the school for some years to come....

April, 1955

I am busy building a new addition to the church here at Lundi. Our people can't all get in on Sundays. Also, I am starting a building at the Clinic for outpatients. Had a good Quarterly Meeting last Sunday about forty miles from here. District Quarterly Meeting about ten miles away over May 1, then Conference at Chikombedzi over May 15....

July, 1955

Next week I will finish four weeks of school with most of my evangelists. I have had them here at the mission station. I am very much pleased with the results and feel that the time taken has been profitably spent.

Ralph was still vigorous and strong, but Ethel's arthritis was making life increasingly difficult for her. Not wanting to be a burden to Ralph, she did not complain. But to Mother Jacobs, she wrote asking for prayer. Once she commented:

> ... It has been such a blessing to me lately to think someday we are going to step out of all our infirmities and shortcomings, and all that is earthy, and will arise in our glorified bodies — all through the blood of Jesus. Yes, these bodies must wear out sooner or later, but our spirits need not grow old. ...

Ralph had always said they would retire in Africa, for that had become home to them. But as the time to retire came near, he was not sure. For months he wrestled with the matter, and then, while away on an inspection of outstations, he finally came to his decision. When he returned home he told Ethel that they would retire in America, and they would leave Rhodesia by the end of 1955. By that time, they would have completed their forty years. Ralph assured her that God would give them grace to leave, although it would be hard to do.

From then on, their hearts were torn between the necessity to go and their desire to stay. But they remained firm in their decision.

> ... Yes, I am satisfied we decided right.... When one gets old, I think one is better off among his own people. We had planned to stay here after retirement, but if we should get helpless, then we would be a burden on the missionaries.... I don't face the future with much joy. It means more now to go back and adjust to home life than it did to first come to Africa. Of course, it means to start life from the bottom again — we wouldn't bring much of anything home with us.... I am almost bewildered thinking about it, but we will go when the time comes, trusting God to provide a quiet little place.... I would like to still be able to help

some simple people over there if we can find the right place, but it will have to be the Lord. . . .

Ralph and Ethel asked that no fuss be made over their going, but their missionary family could not let them leave without a farewell. A barbecue was held in their honor at a beautiful spot on the Nuanetsi River. They were each given a self-winding wristwatch — so Ralph would never need to tell time by the sun again, and Ethel could give her painful fingers a rest.

On their final day at Lundi, Ralph and Ethel said very little, then slipped away quietly and sadly, leaving their hearts behind them.

Chapter 7

United States 1955-1970

Ralph and Ethel arrived home in Youngsville, Pennsylvania, bought a house that had been damaged by fire, and when Ralph had reconstructed it, they settled down to life in America. But they had lived too long in the fresh air of tropical Africa to be confined indoors during Pennsylvania's long, cold winters.

The following year they bought a large lot in Eustis, Florida, near Ethel's sister, and Ralph laid the foundation for their winter home. They returned the next winter, and as soon as Ralph had completed two rooms, they moved in and camped while he finished the rest. From then on, they spent their summers in Pennsylvania and their winters in Florida.

Mother Jacobs passed away in 1959 at the age of ninety-five, having been Ralph and Ethel's faithful prayer partner through their entire missionary career.

In the spring of 1963, Ethel was too ill to go north, so Ralph tenderly cared for her until she passed away on December 11, at the age of seventy-four. Ethel had lived her life full and well. She had been a beautiful example of Christ's love to all who knew her. She could meet her Lord with joy, for she had much fruit to lay at His feet.

After fifty-two years of her constant companionship, Ralph was lost without Ethel. For a year and a half he walked alone. Then the Lord lovingly brought another missionary lady, Miss Ila Gunsolus, into his life to share his remaining years.

Ralph and Ethel had first met Ila in 1923, when they went to Franklinville, New York, to study Portuguese. Ila was then a young college girl, but later she was appointed as a missionary teacher to South Africa, and she arrived at Fairview Mission Station in Natal, while Ralph and Ethel were there on vacation. In 1936 she was transferred to Central Africa, but it "just happened" that through the years, their few furloughs coincided. More than that, they were usually sent by the Board to the same gatherings and were housed in nearby rooms, which gave them opportunity to renew their acquaintance.

It was only natural, that in his loneliness, Ralph's thoughts turned to this lovely lady whom he had known for so long. They had not seen each other for ten years when he wrote to ask her if she would take Ethel's place in his home.

Ila was alone in the mission house at Kibogora Mission, Rwanda, when the mail bag arrived. She sorted the post and laid Ralph's letter aside to be read last. To her surprise, it was a proposal! Ila shared Ralph's letter with her housemate. She cautioned Ila to think clearly. She wanted her to accept. Ila knew Ralph was a prince of a man, and, after talking it over with the Lord, she wrote Ralph a letter of encouragement.

She told Ralph that although she could never take anyone else's place, she would like very much to have a place of her own in his home. Of course, that was just what Ralph had in mind.

Ila's retirement was almost due. Ralph had made sure of that fact before he proposed, for he said he would not have asked her if it had meant taking her away from the work God called her to do.

Ila had relinquished the principalship of the Kibogora school a year or so before this time to one of her pupils who had completed the teacher's course with honors. Thus she achieved the ultimate goal of her long missionary career.

By the time Ila reached America, Ralph thought he had been alone long enough. Within three weeks they were married, on July 13, 1965, in Ila's home church, in Franklinville, New York. Ralph's brother, Howard, who was then district superintendent in Oil City Conference, performed the ceremony. After a luncheon provided by Ila's niece, Mrs. Louise Hall, the newlyweds drove directly to Eustis, Florida, and settled in the home Ralph had built.

"God has been so good to me," Ralph wrote to his missionary friends in Rhodesia, when he announced his marriage. "He has given me not one, but *two* missionary ladies to be my wife." His words seemed to reflect the twinkle in his eye.

During their five happy years together, Ila found Ralph to be as he had always been, a home-loving man who lived a busy, disciplined life. His private prayer time was still the first hour of each day. He taught an adult Sunday school class for which he studied two or more hours each morning. He delighted to tend the small citrus grove and garden which he had planted, and there were always buildings to be repaired or painted.

Missions were still his main interest. He assisted for a while in translation work. He sent his tithe regularly to the mission field to be used for the evangelists or some other special need. He prayed much for the African pastors and for the areas that were still unreached by the gospel. In 1959 he wrote a letter to the church in Portuguese East Africa to be read at the annual conference. In it he challenged the people to finish the good work of reaching all of Hlengweland for God. Part of his letter is translated as follows:

> I am happy to hear of your life and faith in the Lord. But I am praying for you. I am stirred up by the Lord to write you this matter....
>
> I see four places that are still in darkness near the village of the Christians.... The church has sat with

the light for many years. But the land of the Hlengwe began to hear of Jesus in 1928. Thirty years and one have passed since they sent for evangelists to open Hlengwe. [Then Ralph listed the four places by name, describing in detail their location, where the gospel had still not been proclaimed and where the people were asking for help.]

See, my friends, don't be slow to sow grain there. The days are evil.... Are you agreeing for the birds of Satan to go before and finish the grain in the garden of the Lord? Arise. Go to the work of God while you have time to work. Long ago you sang, "The land of the Hlengwe is opened." All right, part of Hlengwe has been opened, but have you finished all the country of the Hlengwe? ...

I am not writing this matter to the preachers. They are not able to do this work. I am writing you of the church that you will arise with the strength of God to do the work to free your friends who are bound by the great enemy. I pray for you that you will rest yourselves in the arms of the Lord Jesus. You ask Him, the owner of the way, to go with you. May the Lord bless you all.

                    Stay nicely, all my children,
                    It is I,
                    Mufundisi Jacobi

Ralph kept in touch with his missionary friends by means of a wide correspondence. In a tape, which he sent to the Rhodesia missionaries in 1969, he referred to himself as "Uncle Jakey," and his closing words were ones of encouragement:

... I believe that until the end of the age, no matter how much violence and venom Satan can inject into the mass of mankind, there will be those, here and there, who long for peace and purity that only salvation through Christ can bring.... So be strong and of a good courage, and never give up....

One Sunday morning, at the age of eighty, Ralph taught his Sunday school class as usual. The next day he entered the hospital where it was discovered that cancer had already advanced too far. After three weeks in Orlando and five weeks in Eustis, Ila took him home to care for him. Six days later, on May 21, 1970, while Ila and his brother Howard watched, Ralph looked up as though he saw something wonderful. Then he was gone. Ralph was laid to rest beside Ethel in the beautiful cemetery adjoining their property.

In a letter of testimony to the Board in 1945, Ralph quoted the verse, "Let us run with patience the race that is set before us, looking unto Jesus...." Then he commented, "To finish the race with a good degree of patience is a prize worth striving for." Ralph Jacobs finished his race with patience and reached his prize. His work was done.

But fruit is still being harvested today in Portuguese East Africa and Rhodesia because Ralph Jacobs "passed that way." And God alone knows the measure of the abundance.

Epilogue
1956-1977

The Rhodesian mission, which began with one, lone missionary couple working in partnership with God, expanded until there were more missionaries serving in Rhodesia than in any other Free Methodist mission field.

At Lundi, the medical work grew from Ethel's mud hut into a clinic where the missionary nurse and her helpers saw two hundred to three hundred patients each day and sometimes delivered thirty to one hundred babies each month. At Chikombedzi, a fine, large hospital was established with a nurses' training program. Through the years, multitudes of patients found healing there. And many of those found new life through faith in Jesus Christ.

Daisy Frederick's Lundi Central School is now a four-year high school, providing quality academic training as well as knowledge of a living Saviour. Today three of its graduates and three from Central Elementary School are in America, Canada, and Scotland preparing themselves to return to their country and their people to teach, to nurse, and to evangelize.

The Vahlanganyeti (the Rhodesian Woman's Missionary Society), with at least two hundred members, is recognized today as an essential arm of the Rhodesian Free Methodist Church. It has had the special blessing of God through the years. In 1959, God called Ruth Smith from her teaching position at Lundi to go into the reserves and work full time with the women. This she did with marked success. When she passed away in 1964, Laverna Grandfield was called from her nursing program at Chikombedzi to take Ruth's place. The dedicated ministry of these two women was used to strengthen the church and prepare the African wives and mothers to serve the Lord.

Although Ralph was unable to see a Bible school established while he was there, it became a reality in 1957 after land adjoining Lundi Mission was granted for that purpose. There was no money for buildings or supplies at first; but Eldon Sayre began with a class of fifteen men, most of whom Ralph had seen converted, and taught them during the dry months of May through September when they were not busy in their fields.

A small, thatched cottage served as their temporary classroom. The men slept in the boys' dorm at Lundi school during the week and went home over the weekends to preach in their churches. Every Monday morning, one of the students would return very early to take a turn hunting with Eldon for the supply of meat for the week.

During the second year, the Vahlanganyeti contributed funds to help build a dorm. Then in the early 1960s, a regular appropriation was made by the Mission Board for scholarships, buildings, and equipment, and a full-time program was launched with the Reverend Philip Capp as principal.

From this Bible school have come dedicated, able men and women who are preaching and teaching the Word throughout Matibi No. 1 and No. 2 reserves (now called Tribal Trust Lands) and beyond, even to the neighboring country of Malawi.

And so, the mission to the vaHlengwe has spread from Portuguese East Africa, beyond the boundaries of Rhodesia, and beyond the tribal boundaries of the baHlengwe, to another country and other tribes.

However, as this book goes to press, life in Rhodesia as

the Jacobses knew it, has, to a large extent, ceased to exist. The rise of nationalism and political upheaval have seriously affected the life of the church. The closing of the hospital and partial withdrawal of missionaries have resulted from tension and conflict within the country making areas unsafe. However, the church, the high school, and the Bible school have continued to move forward, experiencing a great spirit of revival. Prayer for a peaceful settlement in Rhodesia should be high on the priority list of every Free Methodist in America.

Some would say, "What a pity! What a waste of all those years of labor!" But the foundation upon which Ralph Jacobs and his fellow missionaries built remains solid, unmovable, alive, and strong. They took more to Africa than white man's tools, a set of new rules, and a bottle of pills. They took the message of Jesus Christ and His redemptive plan for man. That message has changed and continues to change lives. God has not, *He will not* abandon His African church. His people survive and grow.

Today the work of the Free Methodist Church in Rhodesia is being carried on by faithful, capable, Spirit-filled Africans as a victorious witness to the eternal love and power of God. And the future is as bright as the measure of His promises!

SAY IT THIS WAY

Beit (bite) Bridge
Chikombedzi (chee-kome-bed'-zee)
Chopi (cho'-pee)
Dumisa (doo-mee'-sah)
Edwaleni (eh-dwa-lay'-nee)
Inharrime (in-yah-ream'-mee)
Inhamaxafo (in-hah-mah-sha'-foe)
Inhambane (in-yahm-bon'-ee)
kraal (crawl)
Lundi (loon'-dee)
Mabile (mah-vee'-lee)
Malawi (mah-lah'-wee)
Mandebele (mahn-deh-veh'-leh)
Mandumbu (mahn-doom'-boo)
Maranda (mah-rahn'-dah)
Massinga (mah-sing'-gah)
Matibi (mah-tee'-bee)
Mpapa (mm-papa)
Mufundisi (moo-foon-dee'-see)
Nuanetsi (noo-ah-net'-see)
Sabi (sah'-bee) River
Senge (sen'-gway)
Shangaan (shahn'-gahn)
Shitswa (sheets'-wah)
Tambo (tom'-boe)
Tema (teh'-mah)
Umtamvuna (oom-tom-voo'-nah)
Vahlanganyeti (vah-lahn-gahn-yeh'-tee)
vaHlengwe (vah-shlen'-gweh)
Vakaranga (vah-kah-rahn'-gah)
Xereni (sheh-reh'-nee)
Zulu (zoo'-loo)

Missionaries in
MOZAMBIQUE AND SOUTH AFRICA
(excluding Transvaal)

Adamson, Rev. and Mrs. Frank 1929-34
Agnew, G. Harry 1885-1903
Agnew, Lillie (Smith) (Mrs. G. H.) 1897-1939
Agnew, Susie (Sherman) (Mrs. G. H.) 1895
Allen, Grace 1888-1941
Anderson, Rev. and Mrs. A. M. 1908-28; 30-45
Arksey, Rev. and Mrs. Laurence 1927-51
Armstrong, Mae P. 1916-51
Backenstoe, Dr. and Mrs. W. A. 1903-32
Barnes, Dr. Harriet (Sheldon) 1909-13
Bennett, Rev. and Mrs. J. D. 1888-89
Bohall, Nellie (Reed) 1905-25
Brodhead, Rev. and Mrs. J. P. 1898-1923
Brouard, Katherine (Gillaspie) 1965-71
Bullock, Rev. and Mrs. Gerald 1922-25
Caldwell, Rev. and Mrs. William 1919-26
Campbell, LaVerna 1947-51
Carter, Florence, R.N. 1948-75
Clemens, Rev. and Mrs. Edwin 1950-75
Clyde, Rev. and Mrs. Elmore 1955-74
Cook, Ethel 1907-09
Cullison, Mr. and Mrs. Philip 1964-73
Current, Mary, R.N. 1945-
Davis, Dr. and Mrs. Arthur 1965-70
DeMille, Rev. and Mrs. Wesley 1937-1947
Desh, Mr. and Mrs. Frank 1892-98
Dickinson, Edna Mae (Hoyt) (Mrs. Merrill) 1939-69
Dickinson, Merrill 1948-69
Embree, Dr. and Mrs. Paul 1969-71
Folkestad, Rev. and Mrs. Robert 1973-76

Frederick, Daisy 1922-40
Gaudin, Lydia, R.N. 1918-32
Ghormley, Rev. and Mrs. N. B. 1906-26
Grandfield, Laverna 1956-62
Gray, Mr. and Mrs. W. C. 1900-03
Grisson, Kathryn (Smith), R.N. 1947-75
Guyer, Mr. and Mrs. Dean 1972-75
Haight, Gertrude 1947-63
Haley, A. E. 1904-51
Haley, Esther (Hamilton) (Mrs. J. W.) 1905-34
Haley, J. W. 1902-34
Haley, Matilda (Mrs. A. E.) 1905-47
Hampp, Alice (Evans) 1915-22
Harriff, Lillian, R.N. 1963-75
Hartman, Lucy 1898-1950
Haviland, Mr. and Mrs. J. J. 1892-97
Hessler, Kathryn, R.N. 1955-76
Hoffman, Dr. and Mrs. Howard 1964-67
Hoffman, Rev. and Mrs. William 1919-24
Horwood, Lily 1947-75
Houser, Rev. and Mrs. Tillman 1963-64
Jacobs, Ila (Gunsolus) (Mrs. Ralph) 1929-36
Jacobs, Rev. and Mrs. (Ethel) Ralph 1915-38
Johnson, Rev. and Mrs. Warren 1951-
Kaufmann, Dr. and Mrs. Kenneth 1976-
Kelley, Rev. and Mrs. Walter 1885-86
Kessel, Rev. and Mrs. G. G. 1908-17
Kline, Rev. and Mrs. Philip 1953-61
Kragerud, Mr. Ole 1907-17
Kresge, Mr. and Mrs. Luther 1945-54
LaBarre, Margaret 1906-07; 1937-50
Larkan, Mamie (Matson) 1947-59
Latshaw, Adelaide 1920-50
Lincoln, Mr. and Mrs. Arthur 1888
Macy, Rev. and Mrs. Victor 1936-74
Madgwick, LaVerna (Campbell) 1947-54
Mudge, Dr. and Mrs. Kenneth 1972-77
Newton, Luella 1908-17

Nickel, Margaret 1902-34
Noyes, Rev. and Mrs. A. D. 1885-98
Palmer, Dr. Marguerite 1955-75
Pine, Rev. and Mrs. Gilbert 1916-21
Rice, Rev. James S. 1913-42
Rice, Dr. and Mrs. Lowell 1941-63
Rice, Mabel (Mrs. James S.) 1913-50
Riley, Rev. and Mrs. John 1947-57
Roushey, Rev. and Mrs. Herbert 1926-32
Rusher, Mabel, R.N. 1969-72
Ryff, Ethel (Davey) (Mrs. Jules) 1918-49
Ryff, Mr. and Mrs. Frederic 1948-53; 1972-74
Ryff, Lilla (Eva) (Mrs. Jules) 1904-20
Ryff, Rev. Jules 1903-53
Samuelson, Rev. and Mrs. David 1973-76
Santmier, Martha (Smith) (Harris) 1902-05
Schlosser, Rev. George 1906-08
Shemeld, Rev. and Mrs. Robert 1885-93
Slosser, Georgia, R.N. 1950-70
Smith, Rev. and Mrs. Carroll 1902-27
Smith, Mr. and Mrs. Nathaniel 1902-05
Spalding, Mrs. Ida (Heffner) 1888-93
Thomas, Dr. and Mrs. Theodore 1931-37
Thuline, Dr. and Mrs. Dale 1976-
Tite, Verna 1947-75
Vought, Naomi, R.N. 1965-74
Weaver, Ida (Rice) 1912-21
Wells, Mr. and Mrs. E. H. 1911-15
Woods, Rev. and Mrs. W. S. 1905-26
Zimmerman, Ruth (Moreland), R.N. 1923-28

Missionaries in
RHODESIA

Abbey, Mr. and Mrs. Alger 1976-77
Beckelhymer, Beth 1972-
Capp, Rev. and Mrs. Philip 1958-76
Curtis, Frances (Folsom) 1949-56
DeMille, Mr. and Mrs. Clarke 1958-75
Detwiler, Nina, R.N. 1947-52; 1955-62
Embree, Dr. and Mrs. Paul 1954-68
Frederick, Daisy 1940-46
Grandfield, Laverna 1963-75
Grantier, Donna 1958-60
Guyer, Mr. and Mrs. Dean 1975-76
Haight, Gertrude 1971-77
Hicks, Dr. and Mrs. Floyd 1971-73
Houser, Rev. and Mrs. Tillman 1948-
Hurd, Dr. and Mrs. Lionel 1966-76
Jacobs, Rev. and Mrs. (Ethel) Ralph 1938-57
Kuhn, Dr. Esther 1961-63; 68-71
Lake, Gayle (Hershberger) 1963-76
Lindsay, Gayle 1969-75
Magee, Mr. and Mrs. Robert 1958-73
Morris, Ruth, R.N. 1952-76
Mudge, Dr. and Mrs. Kenneth 1963-70
Nordquist, Barbara (Russell) 1966-75
Pettengill, Dr. Naomi 1950-58
Platt, Eleanor (Russell) 1972-75
Ryff, Mr. and Mrs. Frederic 1975-76
Ryff, Ruth, R.N. 1952-57
Sayre, Rev. and Mrs. Eldon 1946-76
Smith, Ruth 1944-64
Strait, Virginia, R.N. 1948-77
Weichner, Myrna (Bedell) 1968-74